# Blood Covenant with Destiny

# Blood Covenant with Destiny

## The Babylonian Talmud, the Jewish Kabbalah, and the Power of Prophecy

## TEXE MARRS

**RCP** RiverCrest Publishing
1708 Patterson Road • Austin, Texas 78733

## ACKNOWLEDGEMENTS

My staff deserves maximum praise for their outstanding contributions. Included: Michelle Powell, business administrator, Sandra Myers, publishing and art; Jerry Barrett, computer and internet; Nelson Sorto, shipping and facilities manager; and Steve Reilly, administration and shipping. To my wife and confidant, Wanda Marrs, goes all my love and gratefulness.

*Blood Covenant With Destiny: The Babylonian Talmud, the Jewish Kabbalah, and the Power of Prophecy*

Copyright © 2018 by Texe Marrs. Published by RiverCrest Publishing, 1708 Patterson Road, Austin, Texas 78733.

All rights reserved. No part of this publication may be reproduced, stored in a retrieval system or transmitted in any form by any means, electronic, mechanical, photocopy, recording, or otherwise, without the prior permission of the publisher, except as provided by USA copyright law. The author and publisher have taken great care to abide by copyright law in preparing this book. Please notify the publisher of any inadvertent omission, and correction will be made at the earliest opportunity. Photos and illustrations and the rights thereto remain the property of the original sources and are used here only as provided by USA copyright law.

All Scripture quotations are from the King James Version of the Holy Bible

Cover design: Sandra Myers and Texe Marrs

Printed in the United States of America

Library of Congress Catalog Card Number 2017947365

Categories:    1. Judaism            2. Occult/New Age
               3. Religion           4. Political Science
               5. Current Events

ISBN 978-1-930004-10-8

*The Second Coming*

Turning and turning in the widening gyre
The falcon cannot hear the falconer;
Things fall apart; the centre cannot hold;
Mere anarchy is loosed upon the world,
The blood-dimmed tide is loosed, and everywhere
The ceremony of innocence is drowned;
The best lack all conviction, while the worst
Are full of passionate intensity.

Surely some revelation is at hand;
Surely the Second Coming is at hand.
The Second Coming! Hardly are those words out
When a vast image out of Spiritus Mundi
Troubles my sight: a waste of desert sand;
A shape with lion body and the head of a man,
A gaze blank and pitiless as the sun,
Is moving its slow thighs, while all about it
Wind shadows of the indignant desert birds.

The darkness drops again but now I know
That twenty centuries of stony sleep
Were vexed to nightmare by a rocking cradle,
And what rough beast, its hour come round at last,
Slouches towards Bethlehem to be born?

—William Butler Yeats, 1919

# Other Books By Texe Marrs

Hell's Mirror: Global Empire of the Illuminati Builders
Holy Serpent of the Jews: The Rabbis Secret Plan for Satan to Crush Their Enemies and Vault the Jews to Global Dominion
Feast of the Beast
The Destroyer: The Antichrist Is At Hand
Churches and Pastors Gone Wild!: America's Christian Establishment Has Gone Berserk!
DNA Science and the Jewish Bloodline
Robot Alchemy: Androids, Cyborgs, and the Magic of Artificial Life
Conspiracy of the Six-Pointed Star: Eye-opening Revelations and Forbidden Knowledge About Israel, the Jews, Zionism, and the Rothschilds
Conspiracy World: A Truthteller's Compendium of Eye-Opening Revelations and Forbidden Knowledge
Mysterious Monuments: Encyclopedia of Secret Illuminati Designs, Masonic Architecture, and Occult Places
Codex Magica: Secret Signs, Mysterious Symbols and Hidden Codes of the Illuminati
Mystery Mark of the New Age: Satan's Design for World Domination
Days of Hunger, Days of Chaos
Project L.U.C.I.D.: The Beast 666 Universal Human Control System
Circle of Intrigue: The Hidden Inner Circle of the Global Illuminati Conspiracy
Dark Majesty: The Secret Brotherhood and the Magic of a Thousand Points of Light
Millennium: Peace, Promises, and the Day They Take Our Money Away
New Age Cults and Religions
Dark Secrets of the New Age

# Other Books By RiverCrest Publishing

Matrix of Gog: From the Land of Magog Came the Khazars to Destroy and Plunder, *by Daniel Patrick*
Synagogue of Satan, *by Andrew Carrington Hitchcock*
New Age Lies to Women, *by Wanda Marrs*
Bohemian Grove: Cult of Conspiracy, *by Mike Hanson*
Behind Communism, *by Frank L. Britton*

# For More Information

For a complete catalog of books, tapes, and videos about the Illuminati, secret societies, occultism, Bible prophecy, conspiracy and related topics, and for a free sample of Texe Marrs' informative newsletter, *Power of Prophecy*, please phone toll-free 1-800-234-9673, or write to: RiverCrest Publishing, 1708 Patterson Rd, Austin, Texas 78733. For additional information we highly recommend the following websites:

*www.powerofprophecy.com & www.conspiracyworld.com*

# Table of Contents

| | |
|---|---|
| INTRODUCTION—Watchman, What of the Night? | 9 |
| Chapter 1: Meah Shearim—A Hundred Gates to Hell | 23 |
| Chapter 2: A Covenant With Death | 39 |
| Chapter 3: The Jewish Plan to Seize World Power | 49 |
| Chapter 4: Out of the Pit of Hell—Earthly Jerusalem as "Sodom and Egypt" | 57 |
| Chapter 5: The House of Israel is Left Desolate | 73 |
| Chapter 6: The Kabbalah and The Illuminati | 83 |
| Chapter 7: "Will You Walk Into My Parlour?" | 91 |
| Chapter 8: The Jewish Antichrist | 103 |
| Chapter 9: True Beliefs of Judaism—The Phallic Cult of Sex Gods and Goddesses | 123 |
| Chapter 10: Solving the Mystery of Babylon the Great | 131 |
| Chapter 11: Beyond Babylon | 139 |
| Chapter 12: The House of Israel—Accursed and Bewitched | 161 |
| *Index* | 207 |
| *About the Author* | 216 |
| *For More Information* | 217 |
| *More Resources For You* | 218 |

## Introduction

# Watchman, What of the Night?

"A grievous vision is declared unto me..."
—*Isaiah 21:1-2*

This is a very special book. It is the first to explain the nation of Israel, the Jews, and Judaism, and their relationship to Bible Prophecy and to the end of the world. The Holy Bible tells us very clearly what will be the prophetic destiny of the Jews. We find, for example, insightful prophecies by Moses, by Elijah, by Jeremiah, by Isaiah, and by the Apostles. Most important are the prophecies of Jesus. Regrettably, few Christian writers report these inescapable prophetic facts, so desirous are they of not offending the Jews.

This book examines the *Blood Covenant With Destiny* made by the Jews not with God but with His Adversary. Here you will find the truth revealed and made clear. This book is for both Gentiles and Jews. It is for all who have ears to hear.

***Blood Covenant with Destiny*** is written for lovers of truth. I do pray and hope that *after* you have finished the pages of this book you will appreciate and understand the burden I have and have had since the moment the idea for the book entered my brain and soul.

### *"Out of One Blood" God Made All the Nations*

For over twenty-five years the subjects covered in this book have engrossed my mind and grieved my spirit. I believe wholly in what the Holy Bible says about the diverse peoples of our world. We can have confidence that God will bring salvation to *all* who have faith in and believe in Jesus Christ, whether they are Jew or Gentile.

The Jewish religion teaches a doctrine that is far different than that of the Bible. The Jews interpret the words of the Bible through their most holy and sacred books, the *Babylonian Talmud* and the *Kabbalah*, both written not by God but by the rabbis and sages. These books depict a glorious future for the Jews. They claim the Jews will dominate the earth and heap vast treasures and money to their blessed nation. All Gentiles who rebel shall be beheaded. In their Talmud, it is said that the blood and flesh of a Jew is essentially different than that of Gentiles. Thus, Jews are claimed to be a superior race.

What does the Bible say? In the book of *Acts* in the New Testament, we are told that God made all the peoples on the face of planet earth: *"And hath made of one blood all nations."* In *Genesis* we find that all of humanity proceeded forth from the progeny of one couple, Adam and Eve.

So we are all blood and DNA related, are we not? Why, then, should any of us boast that we are, by flesh and blood, more superior than our fellow man? For that matter, what right does one specific race have for claiming that it is spiritually elevated and more "divine" than others?

Even if we could prove that one race or one color or type is higher in one or more capacities, we would still have to contend with the fact that the scriptures—in which I wholly believe—instruct us that the body of each of us is doomed over time to deteriorate and return to dust. Flesh and blood, the Holy Bible says, cannot enter the kingdom of heaven. Jesus Himself taught that to enter the kingdom of heaven, a person must be *"born again in spirit and in truth."* A person must be transformed and renewed and become a "new creature," and this is a *spiritual* rebirth.

To insure that we stubborn and prideful human beings get the message and cease our boasting of our fleshly potential, over and over the scriptures emphasize that *"whosoever will"* may come and drink of the living waters that are poured out freely on all mankind by a loving God.

Imagine: *"Whosoever!"* There is no distinction or pride of race, ethnicity, or national origin in this universal and miraculous invitation to a joyous eternal destiny.

### *God No Respecter of Persons*

As for the Jews' contention that they alone are "God's Chosen People," in the scriptures is abundant documentation that this is a gross misstatement of truth. The scriptures make clear—and this is irrefutable—that God is no respecter of persons. He is not a racist. Thus, in the letter to the Galatians, the Apostle Paul emphasizes that salvation and chosenness is by grace (the love of God) and by faith in Jesus Christ. He further explains that in regard to salvation and chosenness it does not matter to God if a person is Jew or Gentile, free or bond, male or female.

The one thing that God considers—the one, solitary factor is in *whom* do you believe and have faith that He is Lord and Saviour?

*"And if ye be Christ's,"* writes Paul, *"then are ye Abraham's seed and heirs according to the promise" (Galatians 3:26-29).*

This ends for me—and it should for all men and women—the futile and unfruitful discussion about which physical race is more beloved by God or which is His Chosen race. I therefore say to racists and DNA supremacists everywhere: *"Shut up and leave me alone!"* I do not wish to entertain your devilish theories about racial superiority. That goes for Black Supremacists, Oriental Supremacists, Hispanic Supremacists, White Supremacists, and *yes, absolutely*, for Jewish Supremacists!

### *My Goal: Destroy the Poisonous Fruit of Jewish Supremacy*

I declare, then, that one of my chief goals in writing this book is to suppress, and if it were possible, to *destroy* the poisonous fruit of racial supremacy, and particularly of Jewish Supremacy.

Of all the diseased schools of racial supremacism, I am convinced that the Jewish specimen is the most evil and most threatening to the lives, bodies, and eternal destinies of humankind. Any and all forms of "isms" bear watching and are dangerous, including Communism, Fascism, Nazism, Monopolistic Capitalism, and others as well. But the most satanic and depraved of these is undoubtedly *Zionism.*

In fact, the racial and nationalistic ideology of Zionism has spawned many other "isms," most notably the treacherous and bloody movement known as "Communism" which, in its early stages, was called "Bolshevism" or simply "Socialism." (The Communists themselves sometimes attempted to push the idea that their depraved system fostered the more haughty concept of "Democratic Socialism," an oxymoron if there ever was one).

Zionism has existed as a satanic ideological force in opposition to all things good and even to life itself for three thousand years. But in the 20th century, Zionism's influence in the invention of Communism in all its mutant offshoots—Soviet, Chinese, Cambodian, Vietnamese, Cuban, etc.—was responsible for no less than 250 million murders and untold numbers of tortures, misery and suffering. Never has one system of belief or one people engendered and caused such disastrous tumult and blood. Never in all the annals of human history.

Zionism and its accompanying religious disease, Judaism, are the champions of all time in terms of the total number of innocent men, women, and children being imprisoned in concentration camps, beaten, bludgeoned, raped, robbed, humiliated, and unmercifully slaughtered. The influence of Zionism and its ideological perpetration of criminality has brought an unbearable toll of inhumanity and barbarism to this planet and its people.

We cannot and must not allow these crimes to continue. There can be no peace and no coexistence with such a monstrous and overwhelmingly heinous system as is Zionism. Its practitioners, its enablers, its advocates, its high priests must be bravely and decisively confronted in every nook and cranny where they are found.

### *A Watchman on the Wall*

This, then, is another goal I have in researching, writing, and publishing **Blood Covenant With Destiny**. God has declared to me a *"grievous vision" (Isaiah 21:1-2)*. He has set me a watchman on the wall, and He asked of me, *"Watchman, what of the night?" (Isaiah 21: 5-6;11)*.

In my "grievous vision," I see future history unfolded, and a great serpent rising up out of the bottomless pit. His name in Hebrew is *Abaddon, the Destroyer*, and he is accompanied by so many demonic entities and horrendous night creatures that their number cannot be accurately guessed at. With these, the great serpent goes forth to spread it's constricting body and bulk across the circular globe called Earth. The serpent's slithering journey ends only after the entire planet is locked within its terrible coils and his ugly and terrible head has reached its ultimate destination: Bethlehem and Jerusalem.

I am reminded of the frightful verses of the noted British poet and writer whose pen gave us the momentous image of the beast slouching toward Bethlehem:

> "Surely some revelation is at hand;
> Surely, the Second Coming is at hand.
> The Second Coming! Hardly are those words out
> When a vast image out of Spiritus Mundi
> Troubles my sight...
>
> And what rough beast, its hour come round at last,
> Slouches toward Bethlehem to be born?"

Yes, this is the same noisome, hurtful, and cunning beast I see in my grievous vision. I find him not only in the works of William Butler Yeats but in the books of the Talmud and the Kabbalah, but more importantly, in the prophetic books given us by God, in Daniel, Isaiah, Ezekiel, and especially in Revelation. He is real and he brings death.

Humanity has long had a rendezvous with this cruel beast. We cannot as it were, escape his clutches, his fiery breath, his fury, his psychopathic and barbaric criminal insanity. He looms on the immediate horizon; his yellow eyes are locked on ours as he crouches, lumbers, and slithers toward us. We are reminded of all the beasts that have ever visited our troubled imagination. He is the epitome of them all—a horrible, ominous specter of consummated evil.

What can you and I—indeed, all humanity—do to stop this prophetically energized beast? Can we delay and impede its advance? Is there some way we could possibly divert its attention or—and this would be marvelous, indeed—either shrink its deadly potential or, please God, meet and destroy it? Can the beast be killed before it does away with—that is, *annihilates*—us all?

### *My Heart-Felt Preference*

My heart-felt preference would be for the Jews to change their hearts, to enjoy a renewing of their minds, to believe in the Messiah and King, Jesus Christ. What a wonderful thing if the Jews who now are full of hate toward Gentiles would repent of their evil thoughts and become a loving and peaceful people and nation. Imagine a world in which the Jews renounced their violence and hatred toward Gentiles, in which the corrupt Jewish banker no longer defrauded the masses, and in which their propaganda organs ceased pumping out the immoral bilge and debauchery of Hollywood, Broadway, TV, the internet, publishing, and other entertainment avenues the Jews now control and fill with wickedness.

The Bible tells us that race does not determine a person's individual destiny. Many Jews will turn to Jesus in coming days and will be saved. I welcome these Jews as my Christian brothers and sisters. But those who refuse the Truth damn themselves.

Imagine, if you will, a Jewish people who actually practiced the Ten Commandments, who refused to practice the satanically inspired, man-made traditions and sorcery of their Elders, incorporated in the evil Talmud and Kabbalah. Imagine a legion of Jews who really do become role models and the Light of the World.

Regrettably, so satanized is the House of Israel (World Jewry), it is simply not feasible that this high vision could ever be realized. The prophet Daniel stated that the prophecies in the scriptures are "determined" in advance. The wickedness of men's hearts will push World Jewry on to its final destiny. There will be no miraculous turning back, no reform. For that we have *"a sure word of Prophecy" (2 Peter 1:19)*.

### *Solutions But No Man-made Resolution*

The sense of fatalism injected by the prophecies as revealed in the scriptures, unfortunately, cannot be abated. The reader may well come up with one or more "solutions" which he finds reasonable and worthy of a resolution of this final bloody crisis in which we see World Jewry inexorably leading the people of Earth. I, too, have solutions to offer. But, prophecy is not a thing to be adjusted, calibrated, and altered. It is unavoidable and unstoppable.

The Jews are on the fast track to their occult fate. They have made an agreement with hell, a covenant with death, and payments on their debt to Satan must be made in accordance with that contractual agreement.

### *Jews Sacred Book: Annihilate All Other Races*

The ultimate goal of the Jews is the *annihilation* of almost every

Gentile man, woman, and child and the establishment of a satanic Jewish-led global dictatorship (the Jewish Utopia) encompassing the planet. This goal is expressed by the Jews in their most sacred books, the *Babylonian Talmud* and the *Kabbalah*.

The Serpent crushing the whole of humanity and all of earth within its mighty coils—that is the Zionist Imperative. This is the cherished dream of the Jewish rabbis and the Jewish masses. Only that is acceptable to the Zionist psychopaths who now have within their grasp a good portion of the people and nations of earth. However, they will not be happy until they complete their sordid mission of total control.

My "grievous vision" is that the world situation will continue to deteriorate as humanity descends into the talmudic and kabbalistic abyss planned so long ago. In *Proverbs 28:6* a chilling reality is understood in which God states a principle of satanic psychopathy: *"All those who hate me love death."*

The Jewish majority hates humanity, they despise life, *they hate God.* Therefore, they are psychopaths and love death.

Whether we like it or not, God has fore determined in advance the fate and destiny of the Jews who reject Jesus Christ—or, should I not specify, the destiny of them *"which say they are Jews, but are not, and are the Synagogue of Satan?"* For we read in *Revelation 2:9*:

> *"I know thy works, and tribulation, and poverty (but thou art rich) and I know the blasphemy of them which say they are Jews, and are not, but are the synagogue of Satan."*

### History of the Jews Foretells the Future

The 3,000-year history of the Jews reveals to us their tragic future. We know that God has at times greatly blessed the Jews. He made of the Jews a wonderful nation, He brought them out of Egypt and gave them the Promised Land. When the people of the House of Israel were faithful to God, they prospered and their nation was strengthened. But, the Bible records, the nation of Israel broke the Covenant God had made with them. They even persecuted and killed the prophets sent to them and, eventually, slew the very Son of God, Jesus Christ.

> *"Wherefore ye be witnesses unto yourselves, that ye are the children of them which killed the prophets...O Jerusalem, Jerusalem, thou that killest the prophets, and stonest them which are sent unto thee..."*
> —*Mathew 28:33,37*

> *"Wherefore, behold, I send unto you prophets, and wise men, and scribes; and some of them you shall kill and crucify; and some of them shall ye scourge in your synagogues, and persecute them from city to city..."*
> —*Matthew 23: 34-35*

### They Sacrificed Their Children to Moloch

At times, the Jews became so wicked that they horribly sacrificed their own children to Moloch, the heinous god of fire and destruction.

> *"Then God turned, and gave them up to worship the host of heaven (devils)...yea, ye took up the tabernacle of Moloch, and the star of your god, Remphan, figures which ye made to worship them...*
> —*Acts 7: 42-43*

### Their Barbaric Behavior Escalates

Having killed Jesus, the unrepentant Jews rebelled against Rome and became bloody murderers and terrorists throughout the Empire. Edward Gibbon, in, *The History of the Decline and Fall of the Roman Empire*, speaks of the horrors of the angry Jews who rebelled, atrociously, murdering the inhabitants of the

Empire in Africa and Europe, even tearing out and eating their intestines and limbs. The Apostle Paul, observing the ferocity of his fellow Jews, wrote that the Jews, *"both killed the Lord Jesus, and their own prophets, and have persecuted us; and they please not God, and are contrary to all men."*

Paul goes on to say that because of their hatred and their grievous sins, *"the wrath (of God) is come upon them to the uttermost" (I Thessalonians 2:15-16)*.

Still, the Jews continued in their wicked ways. Remaining a separate nation during the Diaspora, history tells us that the crypto-Jewish leaders of Turkey were responsible in 1908 for the Armenian Christian genocide in which over one and one-half million innocents were massacred.

Later, in 1917, Jews Vladimir Lenin and Leon Trotsky brought the dreadful Communist Revolution to Russia. According to historian Aleksander Solzhenitsyn, over 66 million perished in the gulags and through bullets, hangings, and other bloodshed.

Rabbi Harry Waton, in his authoritative book, *A Program for All Jews and Answer to All Anti-Semites* believed that Communism would be the end-all for the triumphant Jewish victors:

> "It is not an accident that Judaism gave birth to Marxism, and it is not an accident that the Jews readily took up Marxism. This was in perfect accord with the progress of Judaism and the Jews...The Communist soul is the soul of Judaism...the triumph of Communism was the triumph of Judaism."

The world famous Rabbi, Stephen Wise, likewise proudly hailed the Jewish triumph in Russia. *"Communism is Jewish,"* said a prideful Rabbi Wise.

The Communist revolution raged throughout the world from 1917, and endures today in China and Vietnam. By now, some

250 million have been butchered and savaged, all thanks to the inspiration of this monstrous ideology first fostered by the Jew, Karl Marx, and by Leon Trotsky and other Jews.

## *Israel Attacks Peaceful Palestine*

In 1948, the ancient nation of Israel was founded anew in the Middle East. But the Jews had to take back the old lands from the Palestinians who lived there. Their bloody conquest of Palestine is chronicled by Jewish historians, including the Israeli historian Ilan Pappe. Pappe's book, *The Ethnic Cleansing of Palestine*, describes how the Jews, mostly from Poland and armed to the teeth by Russian and European countries, aggressively invaded the unarmed towns and villages of peaceful Palestine. Thousands of Palestinians were slaughtered during the Jewish invasion, leaving scars that last till today.

The Jews have built a huge wall to separate the defeated Palestinian refugees from their now conquered lands. Since 1948, Palestine has been an occupied nation. Israel pretends they want peace, but takes more and more of the conquered Palestinians territories. Palestine demands they be again made into a separate, independent political entity, but their hopes for peace are dashed over and over by Jewish aggression.

## *The New Israel A Military Powerhouse*

The new Israel is a military powerhouse possessing some 400 nuclear bombs and having the most modern attack helicopters, jet aircraft, missiles, and even nuclear submarines. Competent authorities rate the Israeli military as the world's third or fourth most powerful.

Israel has made clear it will brook no opposition in the Middle East. In 1956, 1957, and 1982, wars erupted between the Israelis, often backed by the powerful United States military, and the neighboring Arabs. Israel's war superiority resulted in Arab defeats. Nor were Israel's Jews gracious in defeat. They took no prisoners.

In 1995, reporter Katherine M. Metres wrote that the toll of Israeli prisoner of war massacres grows" (*Washington Report*, Feb-Mar 1986). She wrote a piercing news article outlining the brutal Israeli massacres of unarmed Arab prisoners-of-war. In July 1995, the Israeli press published admissions by Israeli Military officers and politicians that some 400 Egyptian POWs were murdered in that year.

In the 1967 conflict, writes Israeli historian Professor Israel Shahak, more than 2,000 Egyptian soldiers were rounded up, disarmed, and murdered. Their bodies were bulldozed into the sand dunes. Israel Defense Forces General Aryeh Biro, who admitted killing the unresisting Egyptians, justified the deaths. *"If I were to be put on trial for what I did,"* he insisted, *"then it would be necessary to put on trial at least one half the Israeli army."*

## We Will Take the World Down with Us

Such unprincipled brutality is common among the Israelis. This leads us to ask what Israel would do if seriously challenged in the future by foes. Israeli Professor Martin Van Creveld, professor of military history at the Hebrew University in Jerusalem, provides the answer. The Israelis would strike back instantly at the opposing peoples, says Creveld, whether they be Arabs, Europeans, or Americans. Creveld, in an interview says that Israel has the nuclear capability to topple the capitals of Europe. *"We have the capability to take the world down with us,"* he stated. *"And I assure you that this will happen before Israel goes under."*

Currently, Israel sits confident of its military superiority, but prides itself on its diplomatic victories over the United States. It has maneuvered the United States, its longtime ally, into war after war in the Middle East, against Libya, Iraq, Somalia, Yemen, Syria, etc. Israel has even used American money to have built the largest embassy in the whole world. This embassy, costing billions of dollars to U.S. taxpayers, has gone up on the banks of the Euphrates River, just outside of Baghdad.

Observers report that many Israeli commercial firms and military officials have offices located in this embassy. It is expected to become the operating center for Israel in the coming era of Israeli superiority in the Middle East, after Syria and Iran have been defeated.

### *Israel Prepared for World War III*

And so, Israel is prepared for the terrible World War its leaders believe is sure to come. They believe this war will catapult the Jews to global dominance. But what does God's Word say?

The Holy Bible's prophecy points to a totally different conclusion. In this book you will discover what God has planned. God has determined in advance the aggressors and the victors of the coming great conflict and strife. We see, therefore, the conclusion of the matter:

> *"But the saints of the most High shall take the kingdom and possess the kingdom for ever, even for ever and ever."*
>
> —*Texe Marrs*
> *Austin, Texas*

# ONE

# Meah Shearim—A Hundred Gates to Hell

"Woe unto you, scribes and Pharisees, hypocrites! for ye compass sea and land to make one proselyte, and when he is made, ye make him twofold more the child of hell than yourselves."
—Jesus *(Matthew 23:15)*

"The numerical value of the words Meah Shearim, equals 666, which has esoteric and kabbalistic meaning in Judaism."
—Ask the Rabbi
*Meah Shearim*
www.ohr.edu

In the heart of Jerusalem just outside the walls of the old city lies a Jewish neighborhood called *Meah Shearim*. *Meah Shearim* in Hebrew means "a hundred-fold," or better, "a hundred gates." Given the circumstances of its founding, perhaps we should call this place "a hundred gates to Hell."

Meah Shearim was founded in the 19th century by just over 100

Jewish families. They were settlers, sponsored by Rothschild, who signed up to become part of the "new colony." It was part of the wealthy Lord Rothschild's Zionist Israel restoration project. At the time, there were very few Jews in Palestine. The Zionists had big plans to change this. All that stood in their way were the poor Palestinian native population and the British government that had political control of the region.

The Palestinians, the Jews figured, could easily be handled. Ethnic cleansing could take care of that. But the British were a hard nut to crack. It would take many more decades of Jewish money exchanging hands in London, many terrorist horrors perpetrated by brutal Jewish gangs like the Irgun, the rise of Jewish Bolshevism, and two world wars for Rothschild and the Zionists to seize power in Palestine and set up a new "Israel" nation.

Still, Meah Shearim was a start. In the Zionist conception of things, a hundred gates were opened when those first Jewish settlers arrived in Jerusalem. According to the rabbis of Jerusalem, by signing up to emigrate to Palestine and Jerusalem, the Jews believed they would receive a divine blessing 100 times the expected.

Looking back, however, one wonders if this was not the opening of one hundred gates to hell. The bloodshed caused by Zionist ambition and their assault and takeover of Palestine and its conversion to the "nation" of Israel is certainly *more* than 100 times the expected. Indeed, blood continues to pour as the Jews, with assistance from their bully protector, the United States, strive to establish their Greater Israel Empire throughout the Middle East.

Jesus once told his disciples that a corrupt tree cannot produce good fruit. The roots of Israel's modern-day origins were laced with poison from the beginning, so it is no wonder that the outcome of Lord Rothschild's notorious Zionist Plan has been so dreadfully lethal. The tree of Judaism is corrupt in its very roots.

## *Drenched in Satanism and Occult Mysticism*

Not surprisingly, in light of the occultic nature of the Judaic religion, the roots of the Meah Shearim settlement are drenched in Satanism. The founders of the neighborhood were steeped in the Kabbalah's Jewish mysticism and Babylonian numerology. To the rabbis, every Hebrew letter and word has a magical value. They believe, for example, that every letter of the Torah, the first five books of the Old Testament, is numerically coded and contains hidden secrets, including prophetic messages. The egotistical rabbis of Orthodox Judaism and other such mystical sects, like the Lubavitchers, claim that only their rabbinical sages are qualified to divine these secrets.

Would it surprise you to discover that the Hebrew name for the "Meah Shearim" settlement was chosen by its founders because the numerical value of its words translates to the most wicked supernatural number ever devised? In fact, according to Ohr Somayach, an international academy of rabbis and Jewish teachers, the name Meah Sherim was chosen because of its numerical equivalence to the number of the beast, 666:

> "This name was also chosen due to the founder's awareness of Kabbalah, Jewish mysticism. The numerical value of the words Meah Shearim equals 666, which has esoteric and kabbalistic meaning in Judaism, as indicated by the Vilna Gaon (a rabbinical sage) in his commentary to the Zohar."
> —Ask The Rabbi
> *Meah Shearim*
> www.ohr.edu

## *666 A Favorable Number in Judaism*

The number 666 finds great favor in Orthodox Judaism, especially by the rabbis who study Kabbalah. Under the heading, "Number of the Beast," in *Wikipedia*, we are informed:

"In Kabbalistic Judaism the number represents the creation and perfection of the world. The world was created in 6 days, and there are 6 cardinal directions (North, South, East, West, Up, Down). 6 is also the numerical value of one of the letters (vav) in God's name."

The plan of the Jews is to employ the tools of chaos magic—to use deception, lies, money, craft and magic—to obtain their ultimate goal. That goal is the conquest of the Gentile world by Jews and the establishment of a Holy Serpent Kingdom on earth. Thus will the world eventually be "mended" (repaired or restored) and "made perfect." Perfect for them, the Jews, that is. For Gentiles, unholy hell will have arrived on planet earth. The Jews call this end result of Jewish conquest and superiority *Tikkun Olam*. And once again, it is said that, through the power and magic of the number 666, this will be achieved.

The "perfection" of the world is engendered by the cosmic energy force unleashed by the rabbis utilizing the number 666 to work its devastation. Atop the ashes of chaotic destruction, the Phoenix will rise to exalt the Jewish Kingdom. The creative powers of 666, say the rabbis, will bring this about. And so, says American kabbalist and teacher Michael Margolis (who calls himself "Moshe David Ben Schmuel Ha Cohen"), the entire earth is Holy Land. It will be the possession of the divine Jewish race.

Margolis (*nee* Ha Cohen), writes a blog *(seventytwonames.blogspot.com)*. In one of his commentaries, in January 2007, he spoke of the Solar Root 666/Tree of Life. "The purpose of these writings," said Margolis, "is to validate the necessity of the world's religious traditions for the work called Tikkun Olam or repairing the world."

According to Margolis, a proper understanding of the Christian Bible's book of *Revelation* can only be attained by study of the kabbalistic meaning attributed to numbers. The magic square of the Sun is attained by a 6 X 6 mathematical table, or box, popular among occult numerologists. The square contains the numbers from 1 to 36 and its total value is 666.

### *The Force! 666 Involves Pure Solar Emanative Power*

Margolis says that ancient Israel's monarch, King Solomon, was given wisdom by God to understand numbers and divine mathematics. Solomon, says Margolis, knew that the number 666 *"involves pure solar emanative power."* Through sexual initiation, Solomon is said to have channeled the Temple energies—the uniting of the Queen, Mother Earth, together with the King, the Divine Source. The sexual energy and power thus created, he explains, is the key to wisdom, to understanding man's creative role.

"The number 666 is not evil," Margolis insists, although he admits that, "the power this number represents, when out of balance in a person or nation, could be a destructive or self-destructive power:"

> "(666) is the number of the person who is an initiate capable of handling the emanative solar power...In the Asian traditions this is known as the power of the Vajra, the thunderbolt."

In the occult world, as in the Kabbalah, the Sun represents the highest of all gods. Lucifer is accorded respect as the ancient Sun God, and was worshipped in all the Mystery cults and religions as the "Solar Logos." In the New Testament, Paul identified Lucifer, or Satan, as coming disguised as an "Angel of Light."

The thunderbolt symbolizes the creative and destructive power of this Sun God, Lucifer or Satan. Jesus stated: "I beheld Satan like lightning fall from heaven."

King Solomon, shown here reviewing plans fo his Temple to be built, required of the high priests a gift of 666 talents of gold annually.

### *666 Will Bring Positive Change*

Margolis and other mystical Jews say that the destructive and creative power of the number 666 is soon to be unleashed and planet earth and the cosmos will experience monumental *positive* change. According to the Jews, the *"Jewish Mysteries"* prophesy that the signs indicate the closeness of this "thunderbolt" transformation:

"We as a people have entered the epoch where the ability to carry the radiant power, the Zohar...is manifesting. The experience of people on the path of initiation and the signs that are manifest everywhere herald a global movement into the promised son of peace."

We see that according to Margolis and other Kabbalists, the "radiant power," which is the power of Lucifer, the Sun deity of the Zohar, is soon to manifest. Note also, Margolis' mention of the "promised son of peace." This is the one for whom the Jews have long waited.

Pope John Paul II, a crypto-Jew who amalgamated the Catholic Church with Judaism and shocked traditionalists by ending Catholic separatism, issued an encyclical which announced a new doctrine that the Jews' long historic wait for the Messiah *"will not be in vain."* By this announcement, the Pope assured the rabbis that the Vatican would no longer demand that Jews convert and believe in Jesus as Messiah. They could cleave to the Old Covenant and await the advent of another as Messiah.

### *The Jewish Messiah Will be the Antichrist*

That this Jewish Messiah would be the antichrist, the Son of Perdition, whose revealing prophetic number is 666, certainly was understood by the Pope. This tells us that the Catholic Church has by now been totally infiltrated by Jewish occultists and is governed by satanic powers and personages.

This is ominous stuff, but Margolis (*nee* Ha Cohen) puts a positive spin on things:

"There is no gloom and doom here. The comets are the fiery chariots that herald a global entry into the 40 year period called the *Kibbutz Golios*, the ingathering of the exiles. These exiles are all people who are realizing we are home here in the earth paradise."

Ah yes. No heaven. But Here on Earth, *Tikkun Olam*. A wonderful era of peace and universal justice awaits humanity, gush the kabbalists. Earth will be made into a paradise. The solar energies of 666 will be the catalyst for this quantitative leap. Kibbutz Golios is the end objective, a collective of redeemed souls.

This "collective" refers to the world community of Jews, scripturally described as the *House of Israel*. It is comprised of bloodline Jews and the "Righteous Gentiles" who agree to serve their Jewish masters.

### They Follow the Six-Pointed Star

Those to be *redeemed* are the exiles, "the wandering Jews of the Diaspora, who follow the star."

Margolis' reference here is certainly to the six-pointed Star of David (also known as the Seal of Solomon), a star designed and constructed in such a way that its "holy number" is *six-six-six* and its ritual feature is that of the Mystery sexual act—the creation of cosmic energy through balancing (sexual coitus) of the masculine and feminine forces.

This is the meaning of the two, interlined triangles of the six-pointed star. *As Above, So Below*. The male is the rising, or ascendant triangle; the female is the descending "Delta" triangle with the point downward. Their unity, or conjunction, produces the generative force (the "G" symbol in Freemasonry) which occultists and Mystery religionists—including Jewish kabbalists—believe to be the epitome of creative and destructive solar forces.

In the Kabbalah's *Zohar*, the two triangles represent the sexual energy created by the uniting of the Chokmah (Son, or Christ) and Binah (Mother, or Queen). The Kabbalah's Tree of Life presents us a number of deities, or emanations of the

**When Pope Benedict wore the six-pointed star of Judaism on his headdress observers were shocked. The two triangles intermixed have a fertility connotation.**

Divine Force, with the trinity being Kether, the Father and Crown: Chokmah, the Son; and Binah, the Mother. also known as the Shekinah. Above them all is the unknowable and mysterious deity known as Ein Sof and his consort, Shekinah.

In regards to this star, the Jewish rabbis sometimes point to the book of *Numbers (Chapter 24:17)* in the Old Testament, which prophesies: "A star will come out of Jacob, a scepter will rise out of Israel." The Jews interpret this as meaning that an anointed King of Israel will come from the bloodline of Jacob to lead World Jewry into the New Age of Jewish divinity and global dominance.

The Christian scriptures believe this passage refers to the advent of Jesus the Messiah. The Wise Men observed and followed a star, or light, in the east and traveled to Bethlehem to pay homage to the newborn King. He, Jesus, holds a scepter (or rod) of righteousness in His hand.

In contrast, the Jews have worshipped the star of *their* god, the one whom their fathers worshipped in vain while wandering for forty years in the desert. To this star, they made and set up a golden calf idol and worshipped it. In the medieval era, the rabbis once again restored as a significant feature of their kabbalist teachings the veneration of the star. It's sign can either be a five-pointed symbol (the pentagram), or a six-pointed star (Solomon's and the witch's hexagram). Called the "Blazing Star" by the Masonic Lodge, this star is, in reality, the sign of Lucifer, or Satan, who masquerades as the "bright and morning star" and also as the "Father of Lights."

## *The Serpent is the Redeemer*

Margolis' assertion is that the Kabbalah teachings provide the path to initiation not only for Jews and Judaism but for all initiates who group themselves under the power of the Star:

> "The redeemer initiate in every wisdom lineage around the globe is related to the holy Kochav/comet or star scepter. This is a potent sign heralding the era of the great peace in Tibetan Buddhist, Christian, Jewish, Hindu, Islamic, Native American, and other traditions...Shema Yisrael, we are one temple school and orchard—Pardes of trees. A forest of Beauty, Happy and Joyous Tu B'Shevat!

So what we find, hidden among all the kabbalistic lexicon, is the Jews' message. First, he speaks of *"the redeemer initiate"* in every wisdom lineage around the globe. Who is he talking about? Who is the "initiate?" Who is the "initiator?" And who is the *"redeemer?"* In Judaism, the redeemer can only be the Holy Serpent, Leviathan, whom the rabbis honor as the masculine/feminine God of Forces.

Margolis' kabbalist language also speaks of the *"path to initiation"* these initiates are taking. He says that initiates are found "in every *wisdom* lineage around the globe." The word

> Jewish rabbis honor as their redeemer and messiah the Holy Serpent, depicted here in its form as Oroboros, the covering serpent. He is the God of Forces who will reward the Jews with their prophesied Kingdom on earth.

"wisdom" is key, for this refers to men and women into mysticism, magic, and occultism. Judaism is itself a "wisdom" religion and its kabbalistic roots can be traced all the way back to Babylon and especially back to the reign of the apostate King Solomon.

Whereas his father, David, had asked God for the gifts of mercy and salvation, in contrast, Solomon desired *wisdom*. In mysticism and the occultic realm, wisdom pertains to the blessings of the Great Goddess, the gnosis and the hidden thing.

Today, the Wiccans, the Gnostics, and the dark Satanic cults (the O.T.O., for example) are among the world's wisdom groups, but there are wisdom (that is, mystics) adepts in Christianity, in Islam, and in the Hindu faith. The wisdom teachings are related to Jewish kabbalistic practices and dogma which, as I explained, proceeded from Solomon's practice of the dark arts, but also were adopted by Israel from Babylonian and Egyptian Mystery ancient traditions.

### *The Star: Sirius*

We are informed by Margolis that the initiates of these wisdom religious traditions are all related to the holy *Kochav/comet* or *Star scepter*. Here we have the secret "wisdom" doctrine of Freemasonry and the Kabbalah of a coming Star, or comet, Sirius, which the occult adepts teach will align itself in orbit closely with planet earth. The Egyptian high priests taught that *Sirius*, the Dog Star, was related to the cyclical coming of their Sun God (the All-Seeing Eye on our U.S. one dollar currency). His coming would usher in a bloody and tumultuous period of destruction followed by the creation of a new and better world.

The Jews have craftily integrated this Egyptian cosmological myth into their own religion of Judaism. The Star called Sirius is expected to be a sign heralding the coming of the Jewish Messiah and the inauguration of the Jewish Utopia, or Paradise, on earth. This is why Margolis carefully weaves wisdom terms like "radiant" and the "solar force" into his narrative. The term, "Holy Kochav" is directly related as this term means a divine, shiny light.

### *A Universal Religion?*

It all sounds so lovely. But let's decode Margolis' kabbalistic invitation to "Tibetan Buddhist, Christian, Jewish, Hindu, Islam, Native American and other traditions" to peacefully coexist with Judaism and to passively accept the subordinate role reserved for Gentiles in the coming age of *Tikkun Olam*— Jewish rule. This ecumenical call may come across as genuinely tolerant and inclusive, but is it?

Immediately Margolis follows up his broad-based invitation with the deceptive slogan "Shema Yisrael, we are one..." And indeed, the kabbalistic and Talmudic Jews invite all faiths to come under the umbrella of Judaism—to worship in common the "Divine God" of Israel. Thus, the phrase "Shema Yisrael, we are one."

But there is a fly in the ointment. Those of other religions will be required to abide by the Talmud's Noahide Laws. These laws prescribe the penalty of *death* by beheading for idolaters. According to rabbinical law, the worship of gods outside the kabbalistic Tree of Life amounts to idolatry, so Christians and Moslems will earn a trip to the guillotine to have their heads lopped off lest they renounce their "false gods."

The wisdom religions, however, including Hinduism, Buddhism, Taoism, Native American, most African tribal religions, Wicca, Zorastrianism, and others will find their worshippers and devotees welcome. Their dogma, though diverse, does not offend the Pharisees, (Orthodox Jews) and is often praised by the more liberal (Reform and Conservative) Judaic sects. It is the monotheistic faiths, Christianity and Islam, that are despised and hated. They alone are a threat to Judaic superiority.

While the Christian and Moslem mystics—the New Agers and members of the more liberal denominations and sects—will be tolerated, the Jews will strike with all their serpentine venom against the true followers of Jesus and the cross. Nor will fundamentalist Moslems be spared.

The hardcore Zionist aspect of this seemingly tolerant invitation for all wisdom traditions to join hearts and hands is observed in Margolis closing of *Tu B'Shevat*, a Hebrew term which literally means the planting of new trees, but actually symbolizes the Jewish modern-day restoration of the land of Israel and the ethnic cleansing of Palestine.

### The Catholic Church Reconciled with Judaism

The *Novus Ordo*, post Vatican II Catholic Church, which, on the surface, seems dedicated to the Christian Trinity—Father, Son (Jesus), and the Holy Spirit—will for the most part be reconciled with Judaism and permitted by the Sanhedrin, and Chief Rabbis to coexist. Like Judaism's kabbalism, the Catholic Church has roots deeply imbedded in Babylonian magic. Prayer to and veneration of the saints, combined with the worship of Mary, a type of Goddess, is consistent with Judaism's necromancy and its Tree of Life goddesses, Binah (Divine Mother) and Malkuth (Divine Daughter).

Since the papacy of Pope John Paul II, Rome has bent over backwards to please the Jews, even rewriting the official Catholic Catechism. The new Catechism absolves the Jews of any guilt in the arrest, trial, and crucifixion of Jesus; it praises the Jews as "Elder Brothers" of Christians, and presents a new doctrine in which the Jews are exempted from the requirement to convert to enter heaven and are encouraged to continue in the Old Covenant.

These unholy concessions to Judaism are accompanied by the Pope's apology for history's persecution of the Jews in past centuries and an incredible encyclical issued by Pope John Paul II just prior to his death, which explained that the Jews' long wait for their Messiah is not in vain. This is generally interpreted to mean that the Jews are not obligated to believe in Jesus as Messiah and that they may welcome anyone they choose to be their *future* Messiah.

Of course, all these papal concessions to Judaic zealots run counter to solid Christian doctrine, fly in the face of the teachings of Jesus and his disciples, and constitute virtually a total surrender to the Jews and their rabbis obsessed with hate for traditional, biblical Christian doctrines. Because the laity of the Catholic Church has been taught to regard the Pope's encyclicals as infallible and to believe the Catechism's teachings that de-emphasize and delegate the Scriptures to at best a secondary role, the hideousness of this heretical surrender to the Jews is manifest.

All these changes favorable to the Jews were made over the past twenty-five years with only a peep of protest from the people in the pew. The Holy Father is still the end-all for these hundreds of millions of faithful Catholics, and whatever the Pontiff Maximus says is either all right with them—or is at least, grudgingly acceptable. Admittedly, there are a few heroic Catholics, including some Bishops who will refuse to go along with the revised, new dogma. In time they will be harshly dealt with or else dealt with by benign neglect.

### *Jewish Utopia*

So we have the Jews beckoning most other unholy cults and false religions to join their plot to inaugurate a new Solar Age on planet earth. The goal is to achieve the long-sought for Paradise, or Utopia, a time when the divine Jew and Israel have in their coffers all the money, gold, silver, precious gems and other wealth. It will further be a time in which the Jew will be master over the lowly Gentile nations and peoples. This is the Jewish version of "evangelical outreach," proselytizing, and conversion. Jesus surely foresaw this campaign by reprobate Jews to someday attempt to incorporate all the satanic religious groups on earth under its accursed demonic umbrella. He bravely condemned the Pharisees (today's Orthodox Jews—*Encyclopedia Judaica*) and religious teachers, saying unto them:

> *"Woe unto you, scribes and Pharisees, hypocrites! For ye compass sea and land to make one proselyte, and when he is made, ye make him twofold more the child of hell than yourselves."*
> —*Matthew 23:15*

### *Back to Meah Shearim*

Thus we return once again to the meaning of the name *Meah*

*Shearim*, the Ashkenazi Orthodox Jews' first Rothschild settlement in Jerusalem, founded in the 19th century. The legend is that some 100 families settled ("were planted") in Meah Shearim. These religious zealots gave it the name Meah Shearim which, in Hebrew, means "a hundred gates."

The usual definition of "a hundred gates" means that Jews expect to receive 100 times the Divine blessing for their *Mikvah* (good work). However, one wonders whether the name also has another, more esoteric meaning. Could "a hundred gates" relate symbolically to the Sanhedrin's effort to bring into the Judaic fold a hundred world "wisdom" religions? These Gentile religions would be the ones found compatible with kabbalistic Judaism. The followers would agree to be servants and subordinates of their Jewish masters and be forced figuratively to lay prostrate at the feet of their Jewish overlords. Only the true and sincere Christians who belong to Jesus, and the hard-core Moslems pledged to the Koran and to Allah would be denied entrance into the hundred gates.

### *All Roads Will Lead to Jerusalem*

It was once said that, *"All Roads Lead to Rome."* The city's gates were of necessity increased in number but only the unholy entered therein so many were its vices and so huge the city's burden of sin.

In the coming world all roads shall lead to Jerusalem and the wicked will enter the city through a hundred gates. And the hamlet of Meah Shearim shall beckon the unclean visitors on Tishrei 15, during Sukkot. On that day, they will gather and gorge and pleasure themselves, for this is that momentous day when the Star will shine, and the beast shall ascend. It will be time to celebrate the Feast Day of Leviathan, the Holy Serpent, whose number is 666.

TWO

# A Covenant with Death

"We have made a covenant with death, and with hell are we at agreement."
—*Isaiah 28:15*

For many years now I have studied carefully the prophetic books and sayings of the Jews. I find universally in the Jews' own writings only prophecies of great cheer, of a fantastic future as the Jews are predicted to rise up and up, toward their destiny of global domination and worldly wealth.

Considering the many Christian books on this topic, one also finds this same rosy picture of a Jewish future. The average Christian pastor and teacher proclaims the coming kingdom of the Jews upon earth. Writers say that after many deadly delays and fake starts, finally, the Jews who remain will turn to Jesus, whom they have denied for so long. More and more Jews will grow to accept Him, until finally, the entire nation (the whole, physical House of Israel) shall become true believers.

But prior to this rebirth, the Jews will, say the Christians, be blessed by Christ, rebuilding the nation of Israel and being served and befriended by the Christians who adore and respect them.

Some point to the prophecies of *Revelation* and say that 144,000

Jews (12,000 from each of the 12 tribes) shall be saved. Others believe this to be a symbolic number, signifying only that *many* Jews will come to know Jesus as Lord and Saviour.

Strangely, neither the Christian writers nor the Jewish rabbis are eager to go to the counsel of God for sure advice and direction. There, we find what the prophets had to say, and with their words, the very prophecies of Jesus.

### Moses: Evil Will Befall you in the Latter Days

Moses, who led the Jewish nation out of Egypt and to the frontiers of the Promised Land, in his old age gave an astounding prophecy of what would befall Israel. In *Deuteronomy 31:28, 29,* Moses said to the people: *"Gather unto me all the elders of your tribes, and your offices, that I may speak these words in their ears and call heaven and earth to record against them."*

Moses continued: *"For I know that after my death, ye will turn aside from the way which I have commanded you; and evil will befall you in the latter days; because ye will do evil in the*

> *"Evil will befall you in the latter days."*

*sight of the Lord, to provoke him to anger through the work of your hands."*

Note Moses' prophetic words: *"...evil will befall you in the latter days."* This proves just how deficient, backward, and incorrect are the optimistic and bright prophecies given by the Jews and Christians of today.

### Isaiah: A Covenant with Death and An Agreement With Hell

Isaiah is one of Israel's greatest but perhaps least appreciated prophets. He spoke of the coming of Messiah, and his prophecies of Jesus cut the Jews to the heart. The Devil and his servants no doubt hated Isaiah and were angered at his ominous—and accurate—prophecies of destruction. As a consequence, Isaiah was forced to go into hiding. He was eventually captured and his body literally sawed in half by a furious King Manasseh.

But prior to his fateful death, Isaiah sounded forth this ringing endtime prophecy *(Isaiah 28:14-18)* against *"the scornful men, that rule his people which is in Jerusalem:"*

> *"Wherefore hear the word of the LORD, ye scornful men, that rule this people which is in Jerusalem.*
>
> *"Because ye have said, We have made a covenant with death, and with hell are we at agreement; when the overflowing scourge shall pass through, it shall not come unto us: for we have made lies our refuge, and under falsehood have we hid ourselves:*
>
> *"Therefore thus saith the Lord GOD, Behold, I lay in Zion for a foundation a stone, a tried stone, a precious corner stone, a sure foundation: he that believeth shall not make haste.*
>
> *"Judgment also will I lay to the line, and righteousness to the plummet: and the hail shall sweep away the refuge of lies, and the waters shall overflow the hiding place.*
>
> *"And your covenant with death shall be disannulled, and your agreement with hell shall not stand; when the overflowing scourge shall pass through, then ye shall be trodden down by it."*

Please, read again very slowly Isaiah's amazing prophecy aimed at the wicked men who are the leaders of Jerusalem. First, we see the setting aside by God of their deceitful and pompous *"covenant with death."* These evil men had even confidently boasted, *"with hell are we at agreement."*

*"The overflowing scourge will pass us by"* they declared. *"For we have made lies our refuge and under falsehood have we hid ourselves."*

How psychopathic are these "Scornful men of Jerusalem?" How criminal minded!

Isaiah told the leaders that Jesus' coming was *"a sure foundation"* and a *"tried stone,"* even a precious *"cornerstone."* Only he that believed would be saved, said the prophet. Judgement was coming for the Jews; hail and raging waters would sweep away their satanic refuge of lies and would overflow their presumed hiding place.

Isaiah's outrage rose to a powerful crescendo: *"and your covenant with hell shall be disannulled, and your agreement with hell shall not stand."*

Then, the prophet pronounced their pitiful destiny; he said as to their tragic fate: *"when the overflowing scourge shall pass by, then ye shall be trodden down by it."*

### Talmud and Kabbalah are Mute

Imagine, Moses prophesying that evil would befall the Jews *"in the latter days,"* and Isaiah testifying that the scornful men that rule Jerusalem would enter into a vain and worthless *"covenant with death."* Moreover, he prophesied that *"with hell"* these evil men of Jerusalem would be at agreement.

The Talmud so beloved of the Jews does not mention—or repeat—these frightening prophecies. Nor does the Kabbalah note the scary future that awaits. The rabbis who wrote the Talmud and the Kabbalah are, indeed, liars and false prognosticaters.

Many Christians also point to an overly optimistic future, promising the Jews that they will be blessed in the last days, that they will return to build up Jerusalem and Israel. Not only that, but the Christians speak of a wonderful and prosperous future as the Jews are blessed with material goods and riches. These rewards and blessings are to come in spite of the Jews stubborn refusal to turn to God's Son and their gregarious love of and seeking after worldly riches.

The Jew, Karl Marx, the philosopher whose demented brain gave many of the communist doctrines to the world, rightly said of his fellow Jews:

"Money is the jealous god of Israel, in face of which no other god may exist. Money degrades all the gods of men—and turns them into commodities. Money is the universal self-established value of all things."

Heinrich Henne, the famous 19th century Jewish philosopher, shrewdly stated:

"Money is the god of the Jews, and Rothschild is his prophet."

Jesus warned the Jews that they would have to choose between God and mammon (money); for no one can serve two masters.

### *The Synagogue of Satan is Prophesied*

Today, one hears a lot of speculation about the coming antichrist. Many say he will be a radical Moslem leader. They point to the 1.4 billion Moslems in the world and to the prevalence today of Moslem terrorist activity. Only a generation ago, people worried that Stalin, a Communist, Hitler, a Nazi, or possibly Mussolini, a Fascist, would turn out to be the antichrist.

This speculation can be put to rest, however, because the Holy Bible makes no mention of the Moslem faith. Nor does it refer to the Communists, the Nazis, or the Fascists. However, the Word of God does point to the Jews and specifically to *"them who say they are Jews but are not and are the Synagogue of Satan."*

That is to whom the Bible refers in the book of *Revelation*—the wicked ones who comprise the *Synagogue of Satan*. Twice, this evil group is spoken of in two different chapters:

> *"I know thy works, and tribulation, and poverty, (but thou art rich) and I know the blasphemy of them which say they are Jews, and are not, but are the synagogue of Satan.*
>
> *"Fear none of those things which thou shalt suffer: behold, the devil shall cast some of you into prison, that ye may be tried; and ye shall have tribulation ten days: be thou faithful unto death, and I will give thee a crown of life."*
> —Revelation 2: 9-10
>
> *"Behold, I will make them of the synagogue of Satan, which say they are Jews, and are not, but do lie; behold, I will make them to come and worship before thy feet, and to know that I have loved thee.*
>
> *"Because thou hast kept the word of my patience, I also will keep thee from the hour of temptation, which shall come upon all the world, to try them that dwell upon the earth."*
> —Revelation 3: 9-10

Not only is the House of Israel, according to Jesus, "left desolate," it is referred to as the very *Synagogue of Satan*. The prophecies say nothing of a "Church of Satan," or an "Islamic Mosque" of Satan, but *twice* warn of the "Synagogue of Satan," a clear reference to the heretical House of Israel. Yet, going one giant step further, the prophecies reveal that these people have even forsaken the right to be called Jews. The true Jew is the man or woman who has faith in Jesus Christ as Messiah. Others are placed in the category of *"them which say they are Jews and are not and are the Synagogue of Satan" (Revelation 3:9)*

How immensely evil and ravenously depraved must be the people who are of this Synagogue of Satan. They are the ones who constantly blaspheme Jesus, who torment and persecute the Christian. They are the ones whom Jesus said are of their father, the devil and like their father, they are liars and murderers.

Jesus unequivocally castigated the religious Jews, the Pharisees, linking them with Satan and showing their responsibility for shedding all the blood ever shed on planet earth *(Matthew 23* and *Revelation 18).*

## *Jesus in the Talmud*

Today, their Talmud, authorized by the rabbinical sages, calls Jesus a blasphemer, a magician, a bastard. Their Talmud also refers to Jesus' precious mother, Mary, as a whore.

Anyone denying this should obtain a copy of Dr. Peter Schafer's book, *Jesus in the Talmud*, which testifies of these things. Dr. Schafer, a distinguished professor, is Director of Judaic Studies at Princeton University. Or better yet, obtain a copy from Amazon of the Talmud itself, in CD format.

The Jews, over the last two millennia, have wheedled and bribed their way across the globe, becoming well known for their clannishness, their cavalier and even monstrous behavior toward Gentiles, and their crooked and corrupt business practices. They have been thrown out of over a hundred nations. Yet, the Jews still whine and shout "anti-Semitism" when they are excluded from Gentile societies.

Those who have had the misfortune of working closely with the Jews are well aware of their corrupt behavior and lack of business and work ethics. Dr. John Strugnell, an English scholar of the Dead Sea Scrolls, worked side-by-side for over 40 years with Israeli scholars and Jewish officials of Israel's Antiquities Commission. Interviewed by *Ha'aretz,* a major Israeli newspaper in 1990, Dr. Strugnell said, "Judaism is a horrible religion" which "should not exist." He declared Judaism to be a rank "heresy."

Dr. Strugnell, a Christian, was, of course, punished by the Jews for his statements, and he was forced by Harvard University to retire early. Yet, his comments live on and survive the good doctor.

## *Judaism A Religion of Lies and Death*

That Judaism is a "horrible religion" is attested to by the millions of innocents who perished at the brutal hands of Jews in the gulag camps of the Soviet Union. According to Alexander Solzhenitsyn, the famous Russian writer often called *The Conscience of the 20th Century*, some 66 million were ruthlessly slaughtered. The vast majority of Soviet Communist leaders, evil men like Lenin, Trotsky, Yagoda, and Khrushchev, were Jews. Over 70 percent of the gulag commandants were also Jews. Synagogues and rabbis were generally unscathed from 1917 when the communist took control in Moscow to the mid-1930s when Stalin, said to be a Gentile, took office as President and Premier.

Vladimir Putin, in a speech to Russia's top Jews, given in 2014 at Moscow's new holocaust museum, noted this overwhelming Jewish element in the early days of the Soviet Red Terror. He referred to the "ideology of death" which these Jewish agents of Satan had brought to his country.

Today, the nation of Israel, seized in 1948 from the Palestinian inhabitants who resided in that territory, continues to abominably treat and kill Gentile people. The Israelis have built up Israel into a terrible war machine, complete with nuclear submarines and nuclear bombs. The Jewish leaders have threatened to destroy anyone—and any country—that stands in their way. Their goal is a Greater Israel, ranging from the Nile River in Egypt to the Euphrates in Baghdad, Iraq.

The Israelis have, according to Malaysian Prime Minister

Mahathir and many others, quietly conquered and now use both the United States and the European Community as battering rams and proxies for their unbridled war on the Middle East and the entire world.

### *Israel A Supernatural Entity*

How is it that a tiny and theocratic nation of some 7.5 million Jews in Israel and 18.5 million worldwide have been able to wield such tremendous authority and influence in global affairs? Is it not because this is no ordinary nation? No, it is a supernatural entity, led and masterminded by Satan and his demon spirits. Israeli religion is, in fact, the very essence of the *Synagogue of Satan,* and Israel is a small but dark, occultly powerful nation given the Devil's authority to accomplish miracles on the world scene.

The modern nation of Israel, magnanimously assisted by the heretical, confused Christian community in America and the West, acquires more power each day it exists—power to destroy and to conquer. It only has to call on the diplomatic and military capability of its allies, America and Europe, to dominate its opponents and exercise hegemony over them.

What terrible Spirit possesses such a people as the Jews—people who pride themselves on their hatred of the Gentiles, who defiantly rail against Jesus Christ, Lord and Saviour of the Universe, and who identify themselves as none other than the *"People of the Serpent?"*

Is it not a fact that this same Serpent, called the Devil and Satan in the book of Revelation, is their protector and covering? Again, this Serpent is he who will in the last days come up out of the abyss—the pit of hell—with his millions of devils to take possession of his chosen people, the Jews, and make war on the saints and against the two witnesses of God. I refer to the one called in the Jewish language *Abaddon* and in the Greek, *Apollyon (Revelation 9).*

THREE

# The Jewish Plan to Seize World Power

"Judaism is a secret, satanic cult."
— Michael Hoffman
*Judaism Discovered*

"The process of messianic revelation must take place in a subtle manner, such as in a conspiracy."
— Rabbi Joel Bakst
*The Secret Doctrine of the Gaon of Vilna (Volume 1)*

It is an unusual thing that the Jews have made no secret of their blueprint and plan to progressively take over the world, eventually seize total global power, and murder all Gentiles who refuse to renounce their own God and willingly become slaves. How could such a heinous plot be so well articulated—in plain writing—yet almost never be openly discussed?

The Jews present two fronts to the world. The first paints the Jew as intelligent, engaging, pious, and even humanitarian. How could such loving persons and nation actually be cruel, vindictive, and wicked? The Jews are in fact, *doubleminded* and cleverly so. The

Bible says that *"A double minded man is unstable in all his ways" (James 1:8).*

This double-mindedness makes the Jew a terribly implacable foe, for on one hand he makes clear that you, the Gentile, are a primitive, savage beast, goyim, or cattle, while, on the other, the Jew comes as a friend, holding a wad of cash in his hand, smiling disingenuously and saying: "This is for you. Let us be friends!"

Beware the doubleminded man! Never forget, the Jew has a Plan for a One World Order. It will be led by him and his ilk. You are of a different race. You do not fit in. You will be killed. The Holy Serpent dictates, the Jew obeys.

## Judaism is a Secret Satanic Cult

Michael Hoffman, a friend of mine, wrote a monumental book about the Jews and their religion. Over 1,100 pages in length, *Judaism Discovered* is a scholarly tome and its subtitle explains its important message: *A Study of the Anti-Biblical Religion of Racism, Self-Worship, Superstition, and Deceit.* Importantly, *Judaism Discovered* explains the Babylonian Talmud, the prime foundation of Judaism, in very stark terms. Hoffman concludes that *"Judaism is a secret, satanic cult."*

The encyclopedic book is damning for this satanic religion. Here are just a few of the topics it covers:

- The superiority of the Jews
- The inferiority of the Gentiles
- Sexual intercourse with children
- Sex magic
- Ritual murder

The horrible nature of Judaism leads us to go one step further. Judaism is not only a secret satanic cult, it is a satanic cult posing as a religion. Judaism has as its goal the repudiation of all morality and its replacement with base paganism and dynamic evil. Human divinity, group sex, the promotion of pedophilia, the encouragement of alcoholism, they are all part and parcel of the Judaic religion. Judaism is so evil that the three wicked "isms" of the 19th and 20th centuries bounded from its sickening doctrines: Zionism, Communism, and Nazism.

Even the six-pointed star, which depicts and symbolizes the male (triangle) having intercourse with the female (triangle) is coarse and crude. The Jews adopted this star from the Egyptians, Babylonians, and Canaanites. The six-pointed star is exposed as a satanic device both in the Old and New Testaments. Still, the Jews insist on wearing it and it has become a fetish on their national flag.

The prophet Amos pointed to the wickedness of the Israelites, who sacrificed their own children to the satanic star god:

> *"But ye have borne the tabernacle of your Moloch and Chiun your images, the star of your god, which ye made to yourselves. Therefore will I cause you to go into captivity beyond Damascus, saith the LORD, whose name is The God of hosts."*
> —*Amos 5:26-27*

Later, at the time of Jesus, the Christian martyr, Stephen, inspired by God, straitlaced the angry Jews who went on to get revenge by murdering him:

> *"Yea, ye took up the tabernacle of Moloch, and the star of your god Remphan, figures which ye made to worship them: and I will carry you away beyond Babylon."*
> —*Acts 7:43*

Israeli scholar Israel Shahak, in his excellent book, *Jewish History, Jewish Religion*, points out that the fundamentalist Jew spouts vain repetitions, chanting, bobbing his head and thrusting his body because this is a form of hypnotic sex. Nathanael Kapner, a Jew who now is a fervent Christian, says this is called "Davening." It is a kabbalistic practice and a sexual act in which the Jewish rabbi or layman thrusts his hips and genitalia in and out. Such worship is the simulating of sex with the Shekinah or another god or goddess figure from the kabbalistic Tree of Life.

## *The Coming of the Messianic Era: Secret Inner Circles*

The satanic practices of today's Jews are dress rehearsals for the supreme evil that is to come when the Holy Serpent is ready to rush out of the bottomless pit in Jerusalem (see *Revelation 9* and *11*) and proceeds to carry out his Plan in fury. "The final redemption of the Jewish people and global evolution into a higher dimension" will quickly take shape, Rabbi Joel Bakst explains.

First, he notes, "Only with the return to the Land of Israel and the reestablishment of the physical and spiritual center of the Jewish people, could the vision of total unification come to fruition."

The prophetic Kabbalah book, *Kol HaTor*, chronicles what is to occur. First, the redeemer and his Shekinah will be in total unity. Their sexual prowess will have been fulfilled in total restoration.

Next will come the final victory over both opposing world religions, Christendom and Islam. "This will occur," explains the book, "through our efforts to gather the exiles, rebuild Jerusalem, and through the establishment of Inner Circles."

The "establishment of Inner Circles" relates to the Jews' many religious secret societies and pro-Zionist groups, ranging from the ADL and AIPAC, to the hundreds of Masonic Lodges, the Skull and Bones Society, the Council on Foreign Relations, etc.

The destruction of the Christian and Islamic faiths will be overseen by the Holy Serpent and his Jewish Messiah. The

BLOOD COVENANT WITH DESTINY ○ 53

The Kabbalah's Tree of Life teaches that the Jewish people will rise from the abyss with the Holy Serpent as their god and protector.

Noahide Laws in the Talmud say that beheading by guillotine will be the punishment for all who refuse the "kind offer" of the rabbis to become a "righteous gentile." Only those who destroy their idols (Note: Jesus is considered an "idol") will be deemed righteous.

The impure elements (the Palestinians and others) must be removed from the Land of Israel. Jerusalem is to be rebuilt, and the Temple must be reestablished. Once this is done, then the Messiah shall come.

The learning of Kabbalah will quickly occur once the Messiah has arrived. New, esoteric teachings will be revealed. Military conquests will be made, obviously with the help of the Gentiles who are willing to ditch Jesus or Allah.

### *A Conspiracy to Take Place*

The work of the Inner Circles and of the Messiah will be done in secret:

> "The process of messianic revelation must take place in a subtle manner, such as in a conspiracy."

Those initiated into the "esoteric wisdom" will take leadership roles. "The teachings of the Kabbalah...are the very source of Israel's ascendancy and the means through which Israel can achieve the most elevated status...for Israel's praise in the eyes of the world is her esoteric wisdom."

All these measures will bring "rectification" of God's Kingdom and will culminate in the final *Tikkun* (mending or restoration).

Metatron (the Holy Serpent, Satan) will supervise all things. He is the "collective oversoul" who guarantees Tikkun. Every Jew must transcend humanity and grow spiritually, becoming a god. "One who does not ascend from the purely physical remains comparable to a beast."

Tikkun also means fusion of masculine and feminine

**Metatron, the Serpent angel, in human form with horns.**

aspects, both at the earthly and heavenly levels *(As Above, So Below)*. This is the "groom rejoicing with his bride." The Hindus call it tantric sex. Here is how Rabbi Bakst describes this fusion as the end-all for the Jews who are lifted to divinity:

> "Fusion refers to the process of fusing with God's Presence. After one has ascended through the six levels...it is possible to attain to the level of reuniting the Holy One together with His Divine Presence, to experience the return of the Shekinah to Zion and the fulfillment of Redemption."

## FOUR

# Out of the Pit of Hell—Earthly Jerusalem as "Sodom and Egypt"

"And the fifth angel sounded, and I saw a star fall from heaven unto the earth: and to him was given the key of the bottomless pit... And they had a king over them, which is the angel of the bottomless pit, whose name in the Hebrew tongue is Abaddon, but in the Greek tongue hath his name Apollyon..."
— *Revelation 9:1,11*

In the previous chapter, we asked about the mysterious power exercised by Israel in the last days. What gives this tiny, insignificant nation with its small population such vast authority? Its authority over major superpowers is unexcelled, even to the extent that American and other nations have expended thousands of lives and untold billions of dollars in building up and defending the Jews, aiding their obscene aggression toward their supposed enemies.

We attributed this great authority to Satan, the devil, and the Serpent, who is the god of Israel and its recognized Messiah. This undeniable fact, known to the high priests in rabbinical councils but kept from many in the Jewish masses, is carefully explained and described in my book, *Holy Serpent of the Jews*. There is no doubt that the Serpent is the god of Israel who is master over the lesser deities of their Kabbalah Tree of Life and is the groom of the bride whom the Jews call the Shekinah Presence.

Do the scriptures affirm the Serpent is god of Israel? Absolutely! We see, in *Revelation 2* and *3*, that those who claim to be Jews are actually the Synagogue of Satan. As such, the Jews are led to do maximum evil on earth, going so far as to be guilty of killing their own prophets, as well as the saints, that *"upon you may come all the righteous blood shed upon the earth" (Matthew 23:27)*.

John wrote of Mystery Babylon: *"And in her was found the blood of prophets, and of saints, and of all that were slain upon the earth" (Revelation 18:24)*.

Therefore, Jesus and his apostle, John, are united, each declaring the guilt of Israel, *identified also* as Mystery Babylon, for shedding the blood of prophets, and of saints, and of all that are shed upon the earth.

What a tremendous burden is this hideous declaration of guilt? What other nation has been so accursed by God as to be declared the wicked city, *Mystery Babylon*? The greatest tyrants in the annals of history—Nimrod, Alexander the Great, the Caesars, Attila the Hun, Genghis Khan, Mao—none can share with the Jews this monstrous history of devouring human flesh.

No nation can compare to the horror that Israel has brought to the world through many revolutions, wars, and conflicts across the centuries and continuing on into this, the 21st century.

### *Latter Day Terror*

In Soviet Russia, when the Bolshevik Jews seized power and began their genocidal campaign against the majority who were Christians, Jews came from all over the world to assist in the

Revolution. How inflated were their egos as the Jews pouring in to Russia from Europe, America, South America, and Asia took up positions in the government. Torture everywhere was common as the people quickly felt the overwhelming pressure of the Jews' boots on their necks. Solzhenitsyn, in his powerful book, *Gulag Archipelago*, captures the spirit of the times, writing of the tortures that befell millions:

> "If the intellectuals in the plays of Chekhov who spent all their time guessing what would happen in twenty, thirty, or forty years had been told that in forty years interrogation by torture would be practiced in Russia; that prisoners would have their skulls squeezed within iron rings; that a human being would be lowered into an acid bath; that they would be trussed up naked to be bitten by ants and bedbugs; that a ramrod heated over a primus stove would be thrust up their anal canal (the "secret brand"); that a man's genitals would be slowly crushed beneath the toe of a jackboot; and that, in

**Victims of the Jews' Red Terror in Soviet Russia and throughout Eastern Europe. According to historian Aleksandr Solzhenitsyn, 66 million perished. It was the greatest holocaust in human history, but is today covered up by our media.**

the luckiest possible circumstances, prisoners would be tortured by being kept from sleeping for a week, by thirst, and by being beaten to a bloody pulp, not one of Chekhov's plays would have gotten to its end because all the heroes would have gone off to insane asylums."

Solzhenitsyn is not simply being dramatic. He himself was arrested and sent to a gulag camp where he suffered for ten years under communist oppression.

Does the Bible make reference to these latter day terrors? Perhaps it does. In *Revelation 9,* we find prophecies concerning the horrific demonic forces that are unleashed from the *"bottomless pit:"*

> *"And the fifth angel sounded, and I saw a star fall from heaven unto the earth: and to him was given the key of the bottomless pit.*
>
> *"And he opened the bottomless pit; and there arose a smoke out of the pit, as the smoke of a great furnace; and the sun and the air were darkened by reason of the smoke of the pit.*
>
> *"And there came out of the smoke locusts upon the earth: and unto them was given power, as the scorpions of the earth have power.*
>
> *"And it was commanded them that they should not hurt the grass of the earth, neither any green thing, neither any tree; but only those men which have not the seal of God in their foreheads.*
>
> *"And to them it was given that they should not kill them, but that they should be tormented five months:*

*and their torment was as the torment of a scorpion, when he striketh a man.*

*"And in those days shall men seek death, and shall not find it; and shall desire to die, and death shall flee from them.*

*"And the shapes of the locusts were like unto horses prepared unto battle; and on their heads were as it were crowns like gold, and their faces were as the faces of men.*

*"And they had hair as the hair of women, and their teeth were as the teeth of lions.*

*"And they had breastplates, as it were breastplates of iron; and the sound of their wings was as the sound of chariots of many horses running to battle.*

*"And they had tails like unto scorpions, and there were stings in their tails: and their power was to hurt men five months.*

*"And they had a king over them, which is the angel of the bottomless pit, whose name in the Hebrew tongue is Abaddon, but in the Greek tongue hath his name Apollyon."*

### Satan is Israel's Redeemer and King—The Holy Serpent

Is Abaddon not Satan, the Devil? Is the bottomless pit not the depths of hell where he resides? Is Satan not King of hell?

Satan, as I conclusively prove in *Holy Serpent of the Jews*, is the god of the Jews. He is the father of all the gods worshipped in the kabbalistic pantheon of Judaism. The Shekinah is his bride.

*An ancient artist's depiction of the Serpent, the outer circle, and the man of six-pointed star, the father of all gods and goddesses worshipped in the Jews' Kabbalah.*

In *Revelation 13*, we see yet another horrible vision. The Apostle John writes:

> *"And I stood upon the sand of the sea, and saw a beast rise up out of the sea, having seven heads and ten horns, and upon his horns ten crowns, and upon his heads the name of blasphemy."*
> —*Revelation 13:1*

This is Satan, depicted as the beast, amidst his gods and goddesses of the Kabbalah's Tree of Life. He is pictured by the Jews as a Holy Serpent, its body spanning the outside circumference of the earthly circle, which is divided into upper and lower regions. The Serpent, called the Oroboros, is biting his own tail, indicating his idle but boastful claim of being an eternal creature.

The Kabbalah says that this Holy Serpent descends from the highest region down into the lower, which is the abyss, or sea of humanity. From the abyss, the Serpent rises up, which is exactly the scene captured in *Revelation 13*.

The rabbis teach that the Holy Serpent is the Messiah of the Jews. When he rises out of the sea (the abyss), the Jewish people rise with him.

The Kabbalah speaks of two great beasts, one known as *Leviathan,* the second called *Behemoth.* Each is a mirror reflection of the other. Their religious system is doubleminded and dualistic. In *Revelation 13*, we find that the beast that rises up out of the sea worships the dragon (Satan) who gives the beast its great power. The world looks on in admiration of the beast, asking, *"Who is like unto the beast? Who is able to make war with him?" (Revelation 13:4)*

> *"And there was given unto him a mouth speaking great things and blasphemies; and power was given unto him to continue forty and two months. And he opened his mouth in blasphemy against God, to blaspheme his name, and his tabernacle, and them that dwell in heaven.*
>
> *"And it was given unto him to make war with the saints, and to overcome them: and power was given him over all kindreds, and tongues, and nations. And all that dwell upon the earth shall worship him, whose names are not written in the book of life of the Lamb slain from the foundation of the world."*
> —*Revelation 13:5-8*

In the same Chapter 13 of *Revelation* a second beast arises, this one out of the earth. In the Kabbalah we learn also of a second beast, who resides in the wilderness. The striking resemblance to the two beasts of *Revelation 13* is uncanny. This second beast causes all the world to make an image to the first beast. Any who would not worship his image will be killed.

> *"And he causeth all, both small and great, rich and*

*poor, free and bond, to receive a mark in their right hand, or in their foreheads:*

*"And that no man might buy or sell, save he that had the mark, or the name of the beast, or the number of his name.*

*"Here is wisdom. Let him that hath understanding count the number of the beast: for it is the number of a man; and his number is Six hundred threescore and six."*
 —*Revelation 13:16-18*

### The Antichrist 666

So we discover that the second beast is a *man*, and his number is *"Six hundred three score and six."* That is, *666!*

We studied earlier how holy this evil number, 666, is in Judaism. Rabbi Moses Hayesod discloses that this number has prophetic potential. Christians realize, of course, that this is the number of the dreaded Antichrist.

In *Revelation 13:8* is revealed a secret. We have already seen that the Apostle John identifies earthly Jerusalem as Mystery Babylon the Great. This is the Great City which rules over the entire world and is described as center of trade, manufacturing, shipping, banking, and human slavery in the last days. Indeed, today, Jews are at the epicenter of banking, manufacturing, trade, and sexual trafficking throughout the world. In *Revelation 13:8*, is announced the *two falls* of Babylon.

Jerusalem fell first in 70AD when it was invaded and totally destroyed by Roman General Titus. We know, however, that Rothschild and other rich Jews began to rebuild the city in the early 20th century. In 1948 and through subsequent conflicts, the city was further strengthened. It has now become the capital city of Israel and is called the Great City. The Jews are even planning someday to oust the few remaining Arabs that live in Jerusalem and rebuild the Great Temple that sat near where the wailing wall is today.

The Jews call Jerusalem the "Eternal City," but history tells us the city fell to the Romans in 70AD, rose again under the Jews in 1948, but shall fall yet again. "Babylon is fallen, is fallen." Two falls.

### *Jerusalem Sits on Seven Hills*

That Jerusalem is "Babylon" (Mystery Babylon the Great) is further proven in a big, big way by a simple look at the map. Some believe that "Babylon" will be the city that sits on seven hills. This is a misreading of *Revelation 17* which actually says that the Woman, Mystery Babylon the Great, will have *"seven heads."* Verse 9 tells us, "The seven heads are *seven mountains* on which the woman sitteth." Seven *mountains*, not seven *hills*. This most likely refers to the seven continents of planet earth, for the Woman who rides the beast has rule over the entire earth.

Nevertheless, we note that Jerusalem is one of the only cities on earth to sit on seven hills! Rome, Moscow, and Istanbul also sit on seven hills.

### *Two Witnesses Prophesy*

Jerusalem is also that Great City where the two witnesses are given power by God to prophesy a *"thousand two hundred and three score days."*

The scriptures say:

> *"These have power to shut heaven, that it rain not in the days of their prophecy: and have power over waters to turn them to blood, and to smite the earth with all plagues, as often as they will."*
> *—Revelation 11:6*

The identity of these two witnesses of God is not revealed in scripture. What we do know is that their preaching will be endowed with incredible power. Though their public careers as prophets is brief, these two will become known across the globe. Everyone on earth will hear what they have to say, and they will be hated by millions for their testimony. Their testimony will cut sinners to the heart and bring forth the judgment of God.

*Where* will these two witnesses preach? We know where they will be killed—in *Jerusalem!* Yes, they will witness in Jerusalem. The Jews will no doubt grow furious at what these two preach. The Serpent who serves the Jews will be angered as well. So angered that the Serpent will actually see to the murder of the two witnesses. And this murder of God's two witnesses will happen in Jerusalem.

In fact, the Serpent, or Satan, the beast called *Abaddon* in the Hebrew language, will rise up out of the bottomless pit and make war against the two witnesses. Yes, he shall ascend out of the bottomless pit and shall overcome and kill these two men of God. Read these words of God, from *Revelation 11:7-12* and marvel:

> *"And when they shall have finished their testimony, the beast that ascendeth out of the bottomless pit shall make war against them, and shall overcome them, and kill them. And their dead bodies shall lie in the street of the great city, which spiritually is called Sodom and Egypt, where also our Lord was crucified.*
>
> *"And they of the people and kindreds and tongues and nations shall see their dead bodies three days and an half, and shall not suffer their dead bodies to be put in graves.*
>
> *"And they that dwell upon the earth shall rejoice over them, and make merry, and shall send gifts one to*

*another; because these two prophets tormented them that dwelt on the earth.*

*"And after three days and an half the Spirit of life from God entered into them, and they stood upon their feet; and great fear fell upon them which saw them. And they heard a great voice from heaven saying unto them, Come up hither.*

*"And they ascended up to heaven in a cloud; and their enemies beheld them."*
— *Revelation 11:7-12*

These verses are so important I beg you to read them again. First, verse 7 which tells us that after the two witnesses finish their testimony, *"the beast that ascendeth out of the bottomless pit shall make war against them, and shall overcome them, and kill them."*

Next, we read that *"their dead bodies shall lie in the street of the great city, which spiritually is called Sodom and Egypt, where also our Lord was crucified."*

That great city where also our Lord was crucified could only be Jerusalem, where our Lord was scourged and tried by Pilate upon demand by the Sanhedrin, marched by Roman soldiers to the city's outskirts and there, crucified on the hill called Golgotha (the skull).

### *The Beast Rises Out of the Pit—In Jerusalem*

This is the great city, *Jerusalem*, where the beast, Abaddon, ascends out of the bottomless pit, rising to engage in warfare to kill the two witnesses of God, doing so however, only *after* they have finished their testimony.

Today, Christians all around the world refer to Jerusalem in awed tones as that Great City, even as that Holy City of God. They revere and honor this city, they make pilgrimages to its holy sites and pray at its wailing wall, thinking they do God service.

*What a sacrilege this is!* For God has ordained latter days Jerusalem as the city *"which spiritually is called Sodom and Egypt."* Think about that—"Sodom," a city full of sexual perversions and sin, a city so wicked that God judges it and destroys it with fire and brimstone. That is how God views wicked, wicked Jerusalem in these last days.

And "Egypt"—what a description, signifying the false religion of the serpent and the pharaoh, the queen and all their gods and goddesses, the religion that gave the world the pyramid, the obelisk, the sphinx, that once brought His people under captivity. God is telling us that Jerusalem, too, has brought in false religion, even going so far as to worship the Serpent and to create false gods and goddesses in their Kabbalah much like those of ancient Egypt.

Sodom and Egypt—could any other city be spiritually named this? Consider the wicked hell-holes and places of vice across this globe—New York, London, Bangkok, San Francisco, Rio de Janeiro, all are evil and brim full of sin. Yet, none compare with the wickedness of Jerusalem, which God himself spiritually calls "Sodom and Egypt."

### *The Saints Have No Earthly Great City*

After considering these things, do you still hold earthly Jerusalem up as a Great City, a Holy City of our Lord? Might you be confusing this wicked place of consummate demonic energy with the Holy Jerusalem that is in heaven? Yes, that remains the city of residence for the saints of God: *Heavenly Jerusalem!*

We who have faith in Jesus Christ have no earthly city we can call our own. We are pilgrims, passing through, moving on to a much better and more heavenly residence. We must not hallow the ground of this earth; this is Satan's world and we are of God. We are here only for a while, until we, too, finish our testimony as did the two witnesses.

Corrupt Jerusalem is not our home, it is, instead, that city in the Middle East where satanic rites are daily conducted and where blasphemy against our Lord is heard repeatedly. No, that is not our home. It is not a place we should even desire to visit.

> *"And he cried mightily with a strong voice, saying, Babylon the great is fallen, is fallen, and is become the habitation of devils, and the hold of every foul spirit, and a cage of every unclean and hateful bird. For all nations have drunk of the wine of the wrath of her fornication, and the kings of the earth have committed fornication with her, and the merchants of the earth are waxed rich through the abundance of her delicacies.*
>
> *"And I heard another voice from heaven, saying, Come out of her, my people, that ye be not partakers of her sins, and that ye receive not of her plagues.*
>
> *"For her sins have reached unto heaven, and God hath remembered her iniquities."*
> — *Revelation 18:2-5*

God has given us a vision of that lovely city wherein we shall reside. He has prepared a place for us there. John told us about it, in *Revelation*.

> *"And he carried me away in the spirit to a great and high mountain, and shewed me that great city, the holy Jerusalem, descending out of heaven from God, Having the glory of God: and her light was like unto a stone most precious, even like a jasper stone, clear as crystal;*
>
> *"And had a wall great and high, and had twelve gates,*

*and at the gates twelve angels, and names written thereon, which are the names of the twelve tribes of the children of Israel:*

*"On the east three gates; on the north three gates; on the south three gates; and on the west three gates.*

*"And the wall of the city had twelve foundations, and in them the names of the twelve apostles of the Lamb.*

*"And he that talked with me had a golden reed to measure the city, and the gates thereof, and the wall thereof.*

*"And the city lieth foursquare, and the length is as large as the breadth: and he measured the city with the reed, twelve thousand furlongs. The length and the breadth and the height of it are equal.*

*"And he measured the wall thereof, an hundred and forty and four cubits, according to the measure of a man, that is, of the angel.*

*"And the building of the wall of it was of jasper: and the city was pure gold, like unto clear glass.*

*"And the foundations of the wall of the city were garnished with all manner of precious stones. The first foundation was jasper; the second, sapphire; the third, a chalcedony; the fourth, an emerald;*

*"The fifth, sardonyx; the sixth, sardius; the seventh, chrysolite; the eighth, beryl; the ninth, a topaz; the tenth, a chrysoprasus; the eleventh, a jacinth; the twelfth, an amethyst.*

*"And the twelve gates were twelve pearls; every several gate was of one pearl: and the street of the city was pure gold, as it were transparent glass.*

*"And I saw no temple therein: for the Lord God Almighty and the Lamb are the temple of it. And the city had no need of the sun, neither of the moon, to shine in it: for the glory of God did lighten it, and the Lamb is the light thereof.*

*"And the nations of them which are saved shall walk in the light of it: and the kings of the earth do bring their glory and honour into it.*

*"And the gates of it shall not be shut at all by day: for there shall be no night there.*

*"And they shall bring the glory and honour of the nations into it.*

*"And there shall in no wise enter into it any thing that defileth, neither whatsoever worketh abomination, or maketh a lie: but they which are written in the Lamb's book of life."*
— *Revelation 21:10-27*

Now, which city will you choose, dear friends, the Jerusalem that is, gloomy and death-like, where inhabitants are in bondage to Satan *(Galatians 4)*, or heavenly Jerusalem, that splendid city "which has no need of the sun, neither of the moon, to shine in it: for the glory of God did lighten it, and the Lamb is the light thereof?"

There is no Temple in this heavenly city. *Revelation* says, "for the Lord God Almighty and the Lamb are the temple of it."

## FIVE

# The House of Israel is Left Desolate

"Therefore say I unto you, The kingdom of God shall be taken from you, and given to a nation bringing forth the fruits thereof."
—*Matthew 21:43*

Jesus Christ, He who knows and has from the beginning meticulously planned and caused all things that were to happen, has determined the events of the Last Days. And He has told us in His Word of *who* is to betray and hate Him and who shall eternally love Him. He who is the first and the last, the Alpha and Omega, has made it all clear, both in the Old and New Testaments. There are no surprises. This is a sure *"word of prophecy,"* and the book of *Revelation* declares that He is the very "Spirit of Prophecy."

We examine in the Scriptures the evidence for the goodness and mercy of God, how He favored Israel above all nations, how he promised Abraham, the forefather of the nation of Israel, an inheritance and a promise, and how He provided also covenants pledging peace, honor, and greatness forever to His People, of Israel.

### *God's Condition*

These we describe today as the Abrahamic and Mosaic Covenants. He prescribed the Law that the people were to obey. But, always, there was included a *condition*. In exchange for the promise of God which was offered to them, God required that Israel be righteous. He required they possess the faith of their Father, Abraham, and thus be a shining light and beacon to the whole earth.

Throughout the Bible, we find again and again this *condition* declared openly through the Prophets to the People of Israel. And over and over we saw their abject *failure* to abide by this condition.

Today, the Lie often told is that the covenants and promises given Israel were *unconditional*. No matter what their subsequent behavior, no matter how evil and repugnant their sins, it is claimed that God offered unconditional love. Never was this true.

What was true was that God was long-suffering and patient toward Israel. Chastening them for their sins and disobedience, He time and again brought them back into their land. He forgave those who had rebelled. But always, these periods of forgiveness came with a condition: That the Israelites must obey. They must fulfill the Covenant given them. They must be a universal beacon of hope to others.

### *A New and Better Covenant*

Still, the house of Israel fell into disobedience and rebellion. Finally, God sent His own Son, Jesus Christ, with a new and better covenant. The Old Covenant, which *never* was fully obeyed by the people, was eventually done away with. It was, after all, only a shadow of what was to come when Jesus the Deliverer of Israel came:

> *"But now hath he obtained a more excellent ministry, by how much also he is the mediator of a better*

*covenant, which was established upon better promises.*

*"For if that first covenant had been faultless, then should no place have been sought for the second.*

*"For finding fault with them, he saith, Behold, the days come, saith the Lord, when I will make a new covenant with the house of Israel and with the house of Judah:*

*"Not according to the covenant that I made with their fathers in the day when I took them by the hand to lead them out of the land of Egypt; because they continued not in my covenant, and I regarded them not, saith the Lord.*

*"For this is the covenant that I will make with the house of Israel after those days, saith the Lord; I will put my laws into their mind, and write them in their hearts: and I will be to them a God, and they shall be to me a people:*

*"And they shall not teach every man his neighbour, and every man his brother, saying, Know the Lord: for all shall know me, from the least to the greatest.*

*"For I will be merciful to their unrighteousness, and their sins and their iniquities will I remember no more.*

*"In that he saith, A new covenant, he hath made the first old. Now that which decayeth and waxeth old is ready to vanish away."*
— *Hebrews 8:6-13*

This New Covenant is mighty, for not by the law but by the blood of Jesus, redemption is achieved for the people:

*"But Christ being come an high priest of good things to come, by a greater and more perfect tabernacle, not made with hands, that is to say, not of this building;*

*"Neither by the blood of goats and calves, but by his own blood he entered in once into the holy place, having obtained eternal redemption for us.*

*"For if the blood of bulls and of goats, and the ashes of an heifer sprinkling the unclean, sanctifieth to the purifying of the flesh:*

*"How much more shall the blood of Christ, who through the eternal Spirit offered himself without spot to God, purge your conscience from dead works to serve the living God?*

*"And for this cause he is the mediator of the new testament, that by means of death, for the redemption of the transgressions that were under the first testament, they which are called might receive the promise of eternal inheritance."*
— *Hebrews 9:11-15*

God knew in advance, before the Jews were ever born, far, far back in history. God knew that Israel, which His prophets consistently declared to be the "Whore," Mystery Babylon, the Mother of all daughters of evil, would betray Him. Her sins would mount up until, finally, there was no remedy.

### *"Crucify Him!"*

God's long-suffering patience was finally ended. He took from the House of Israel the kingdom *(Matthew 21:43)*. As a last, desperate move, demonstrating His love, God had sent His only begotten son, Jesus, Emmanuel, "God with us," to be the promised *"Deliverer."* With outstretched hands, an aching heart and swollen, tear-stained eyes, Jesus expressed His great disappointment that even though He had fulfilled all the many prophecies in the Old Testament regarding the coming of Messiah, even though He had healed the sick, restored sight to the blind, raised men from the dead, spoken incredible words never before heard, He was rebuffed and scorned by the Jews, who angrily cried out to Pilate, *"Crucify him!"*

This astonishing truth Jesus Himself told in a prophetic parable to the Jews:

> *"Then began he to speak to the people this parable; A certain man planted a vineyard, and let it forth to husbandmen, and went into a far country for a long time.*
>
> *"And at the season he sent a servant to the husbandmen, that they should give him of the fruit of the vineyard: but the husbandmen beat him, and sent him away empty.*
>
> *"And again he sent another servant: and they beat him also, and entreated him shamefully, and sent him away empty.*
>
> *"And again he sent a third: and they wounded him also, and cast him out.*
>
> *"Then said the lord of the vineyard, What shall I do? I will send my beloved son: it may be they will reverence him when they see him.*
>
> *"But when the husbandmen saw him, they reasoned among themselves, saying, This is the heir: come, let us kill him, that the inheritance may be ours.*

*"So they cast him out of the vineyard, and killed him. What therefore shall the lord of the vineyard do unto them?*

*"He shall come and destroy these husbandmen, and shall give the vineyard to others. And when they heard it, they said, God forbid.*

*"And he beheld them, and said, What is this then that is written, The stone which the builders rejected, the same is become the head of the corner?*

*"Whosoever shall fall upon that stone shall be broken; but on whomsoever it shall fall, it will grind him to powder."*
*—Luke 20:9-18*

Then, Jesus pronounced this terrible judgment and declared this awesome prophecy to the Jews:

*"Ye serpents, ye generation of vipers, how can ye escape the damnation of hell?*

*"Wherefore, behold, I send unto you prophets, and wise men, and scribes: and some of them ye shall kill and crucify; and some of them shall ye scourge in your synagogues, and persecute them from city to city:*

*"That upon you may come all the righteous blood shed upon the earth, from the blood of righteous Abel unto the blood of Zacharias son of Barachias, whom ye slew between the temple and the altar.*

*"Verily I say unto you, All these things shall come upon this generation\*.*

(\**Strong's Concordance*—generation means race, ethnic group, or people.)

*"O Jerusalem, Jerusalem, thou that killest the prophets, and stonest them which are sent unto thee, how often would I have gathered thy children together, even as a hen gathereth her chickens under her wings, and ye would not!*

*"Behold, your house is left unto you desolate."*
— *Matthew 23:33-38*

### Jerusalem Prophesied to be the Whore of Mystery Babylon

In *Revelation 17*, Jesus prophesied to the Apostle John of the Woman who sat upon a scarlet-colored beast, full of names of blasphemy:

*"And the woman was arrayed in purple and scarlet colour, and decked with gold and precious stones and pearls, having a golden cup in her hand full of abominations and filthiness of her fornication:*

*"And upon her forehead was a name written, MYSTERY, BABYLON THE GREAT, THE MOTHER OF HARLOTS AND ABOMINATIONS OF THE EARTH.*

*"And I saw the woman drunken with the blood of the saints, and with the blood of the martyrs of Jesus: and when I saw her, I wondered with great admiration."*
— *Revelation 17:4-6*

Who is this apostate, wicked Woman who pompously and seductively rides the beast? It is the same House of Israel of which Jesus, in *Matthew 23* had declared was guilty of the shedding of the blood of the prophets, and wise men, and scribes, *"That upon you may come all the righteous bloodshed upon the earth" (Revelation 23:35).*

In *Revelation 17:13*, Christ calls this House of Israel by the name of Mystery Babylon, *"that great city which reigneth over the kings of the earth."* That it is the same city, Jerusalem, is proven in the very next chapter, *18:24*, where we read:

*"And in her was found the blood of prophets, and of saints, and of all that were slain upon the earth."*

Thus, this is the same city, Jerusalem, as identified in the wording of *Matthew 23:35:* *"That upon you may come all the righteous blood shed upon the earth..."*

Thus, the bloody city of Jerusalem is declared by Jesus to be *"left desolate" (Matthew 23:28)* and is named by Him, *"Mystery, Babylon the Great, Mother of Harlots,"* murderer of multitudes of the righteous shed upon the earth.

### Kingdom of God Taken From the Jews

We see, therefore, that the great city of Jerusalem, headquarters of the House of Israel, is left desolate, abandoned by God. The kingdom of God is taken from the House of Israel and given to another people, the Christians, the House and Family of God. As Jesus pronounced:

*"Therefore say I unto you, The kingdom of God shall be taken from you, and given to a nation bringing forth the fruits thereof."*
—*Matthew 21:43*

The Apostle Paul wrote: *"For here have we no continuing city, but we seek one to come,"* that is, we seek a heavenly city wherein Jesus shall reside with the saints and the host of heaven.

Peter further described the saints of Jesus as the holy nation of God, inheritors of the kingdom reserved in heaven for them:

*"But ye are a chosen generation, a royal priesthood,*

*an holy nation, a peculiar people; that ye should shew forth the praises of him who hath called you out of darkness into his marvellous light: Which in time past were not a people, but are now the people of God..."*
—*I Peter 2:9-10*

### Out of the Pit of Hell—The Synagogue of Satan

We find, then, that the carnal (that is, worldly) city of Jerusalem, is *"left desolate,"* as prophesied by Jesus. And, just as was prophesied, in 70 AD, the Roman General Titus and his troops conquered the city of Jerusalem and destroyed the Temple. The people of Jerusalem were either slain or were taken as hostages and slaves by the Romans.

The history of the Middle East shows that the Jews, being cast out of the city and dispersed by the Romans, never again ruled Jerusalem. Not, that is, until after 1948, when the Ashkenazi Jews, who originally came from Khazaria in the South of Russia, left Eastern Europe and emigrated to the reborn city of Jerusalem and newfound state of Israel.

### Today's Jews Are Not Physical Heirs of Abraham

Frankly, the science of DNA has disproved the Jews' insistence today that they are the bloodline of Abraham, Isaac, Joseph, and the patriarchs. My book, ***DNA Science and the Jewish Bloodline***, carefully explains the scientific research done—mostly by Jewish scientists—to prove that today's Jews are actually not of the ancient Hebrew race. Instead, their origins are in Khazaria, a former nation south of Russia, in the Caucasus.

In his excellent historical book, *The Thirteenth Tribe*, Arthur Koestler describes the conversion of the pagan Turk and Mongol Khazars in the medieval period. The King of Khazaria chose Judaism as the religion for his nation, and forced the inhabitants to convert.

Today, DNA shows that almost all those who say they are Jews are not. As many as 97 percent are Khazars and other mixed blood types. How accurate, then, is the Bible which, in *Revelation 2* and *3*, speaks of "them which say they are Jews, and are not, but *are* the Synagogue of Satan."

The evangelical Christian belief in a Middle Eastern country made up entirely of blood Jews is proven to be a myth. The Jews' belief that their blood gives their race a special mission and a prophetic destiny is also proven false.

## *A Nation Led By the Serpent*

The House of Israel, though left desolate and abandoned for more than 1800 years, was not finished. Its depraved and desperate history had many more years of despair and agony to fulfill. In this desolate state, Christ had decreed the Jews would continue their stubborn refusal to turn to Him in repentance and tears.

So, in arrogance and conceit, under the reign of decadent rabbis and inspired by the Serpent, the Jews continued on, cleaving together, unassimilated within the nations, a wandering city and nation of vagabonds and charlatans. Much like the Gypsies and the Irish travelers, the Jews became a nation unique unto themselves, a hateful and greedy World Jewry.

God, in His Word, describes this World Jewry as bereft of faith and as the *Synagogue of Satan*. He also explains that, in the latter times, these people shall become so infused with evil and so saturated with lies and deceit they literally "agree with hell" and enter into a "covenant of death."

# SIX

# The Kabbalah and The Illuminati

Hollywood is really into the Kabbalah. Paris Hilton, Britney Spears, Michael Jackson, Barbra Streisand, Diane Ladd and a host of other stars have dabbled in it. I got a chuckle out of the recent cover of *Paranoia* magazine that pictured Madonna as sort of a kabbalistic witch. Very clever, and appropriate. Madonna, an Italian-American with supposed Catholic roots, is a big promoter today of "tabloid" kabbalism.

Not only has Hollywood fallen madly in love with Kabbalah. In **Codex Magica** and in my other writings, I have photos of former President Bill Clinton, Senate Majority Leader Harry Reid (D-NV), former House Speaker Newt Gingrich, globalist banker David Rockefeller, U.S. Senator Charles Schumer and horror novelist Stephen King, all presenting kabbalistic hand signs.

As remarkable as it may seem, Kabbalah has even gained a foothold today among many evangelical Christians. Having first embraced Jewish political Zionism, a natural progression has been to move on into Judaic religious practices. Some evangelical Christians now call themselves "Messianics," and anything that they perceive as "Jewish" appeals to them. They wear the Star of David as jewelry around their necks, holy dance in a circle (the Jewish *Hatikvah*), exchange "shaloms," observe Jewish feasts and holy days, and

Former Senate Majority Leader Harry Reid (D-NV) gives a Masonic/Mormon hand sign, the slashing of the throat, and not incidentally, shows his kabbalistic red wristband. Thousands of Jews and Gentiles are into the Kabbalah, as evidenced by the red wristband, which is thought to bring good luck and ward off evil spirits.

enthusiastically quote from the Talmud and the Kabbalah's *Zohar*. As Jesus once said "Father, forgive them. They know not what they do."

### *Roots Traced Back to Babylon and Egypt*

The Kabbalah has Jewish roots that can be traced all the way back to Babylon and Egypt where the Israelites once sojourned and, consequently, borrowed from the ancient Mystery religions in those cultures. *Star Trek's* Leonard Nimoy's famous Vulcan greeting is a kabbalistic sign which is taken from the letter "shin" of the Hebrew alphabet.

However, though the Kabbalah sprang from these ancient sources and was further developed and propagated by the Jews, this evil system of witchcraft and magic is at the very foundation of virtually every Illuminati occult group in existence. Its sorcery is the ceremonial and doctrinal basis for Rosicrucianism, Freemasonry, even the Church of Satan.

The late Albert Pike, Sovereign Grand Commander of the Scottish Rite Lodge, wrote in his Masonic classic, *Morals and Dogma*, that he was "filled with admiration" for the Jewish Kabbalah.

The ritual for the 30th degree of Scottish Rite Masonry is full of kabbalistic trappings. It is called the Knights of Kadosh degree and it comes complete with black curtains, skulls, a coffin, and a shrouded knight from the underworld.

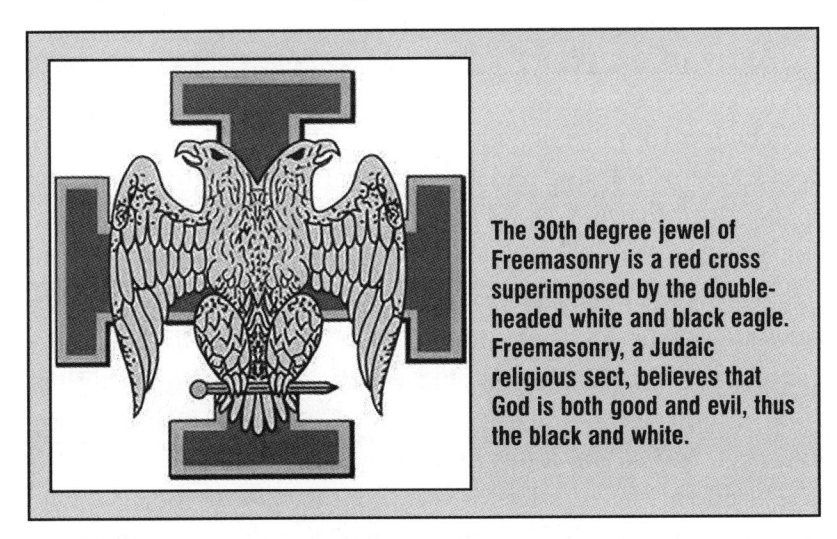

The 30th degree jewel of Freemasonry is a red cross superimposed by the double-headed white and black eagle. Freemasonry, a Judaic religious sect, believes that God is both good and evil, thus the black and white.

Kabbalistic masters spend decades studying the arcane intricacies of the Tree of Life and its hidden, alchemical reverse, the Tree of Death. The Hollywood types merely dent the surface. They are sort of like Shirley Maclaine and her very laughable New Age teachings. The true adepts laugh at Madonna, Britney, and the late Michael Jackson—and take advantage of their fame, celebrity, and money. There are many shysters and sham rabbis around today in the crowded field of Kabbalah magic.

### *The Hidden Depths of Kabbalah*

The wannabes in Kabbalah have little or no understanding of

what lies in the deep and dark, murderous depths of Kabbalah. They do not realize that behind its glittery, gossamer surface lies such malevolent intent. If properly understood, it must be revealed that the Great Work of the Illuminati is being fulfilled through the alchemical syntheses being worked through Kabbalah.

The ultimate objective of Kabbalah, despite the vain and empty denials of many of its advocates, is the utter destruction of all matter, of mankind itself: Annihilation. The Oroboros serpent encircling and strangling humanity. Creative destruction, the wicked satanic kabbalists call it.

Many of the planet's great sadistic mass murderers have been kabbalists—Marx and Trotsky, for example. Adam Weishaupt, 18th century founder of the Order of the Illuminati, was a Mason, a Jesuit, and a kabbalist. I'm afraid that today, the kabbalistic doctrines hold sway in the capitalist capitols—in Washington, D.C., in London, Rome, and Tel Aviv. The neocon cabal is a veiled and shadowy demonstration of it. They actually *want* to plunge the world into nuclear catastrophe and chaos. A fiery chaos and destruction atop which they hope to build their new, occult utopian Order of the Ages. It's a frightening prospect, and so far, it has been successful.

In effect, the religion of the Illuminati is the black magic religion of Kabbalah. The tenets of this diabolical system define the totalitarian political, economic, and social goals of the Illuminati. It is as Mirabeau, during the French Revolution, called it, literally the "Code of Hell."

The religion of the Kabbalah is based on that of Mystery Babylon. It has multiple gods and goddesses, most of which are sexual and phallic in nature. The two serpents, masculine and feminine, who are depicted as messianic in nature, are said to be teachers of the elite. They emerge from the abyss and aid the elite in achieving godhood and mastery over humanity. These two serpents are agents of *Ein Sof*, the unknowable, ineffable Deity, whose real name is *Saturn*. He is the star (six-pointed star). Christians know him as Lucifer.

## *The Illuminati and the Magic of Kabbalah*

What, really, is the "Illuminati?" First, about the Illuminati—this cabal exists in both a real and in a metaphorical sense. There is an umbrella-like constellation of secret societies, orders, and organizations that we can loosely classify as sub-units of *"The Illuminati."* Their specific goals may vary, but the ultimate objective is the same, which is the New World Order, a unified world system, free of godly restraints and prohibitions: *"Do as thou wilt."* In that sense all such groups are allied and are mutually inclusive.

Of course, some are more of a present danger to us than others, depending on the degree to which their nefarious and wicked activities impact our everyday lives.

Using, then, a broad brush, we can say that the Order of Skull and Bones, the Scottish Rite of Freemasonry, and the Priory of Zion, for example, are all "Illuminati;" yet, each has a

*A Skull & Bones Class.* Notice the Masonic hand sign of the man on left and the folded arms of the person just behind the skull. Exactly 15 young men are chosen each year to be inducted into Skull & Bones at Yale University. In the induction ritual the chosen are told that all those outside the Order are "vandals and Gentiles."

somewhat distinctive program, its own regime of rituals, and its own power base. The members of each group may not even recognize the common purposes they share with other groups. Still, we can, with study and analysis, divine common purposes and objectives and often a parallel agenda.

Moreover, many Illuminati have memberships in several interlinking groups. A Catholic Cardinal who is a Mason or Rosicrucian can also be an initiate of, say, the Jesuit Order or Opus Dei.

What we also know is that the Jewish Kabbalah is the satanic understructure of all these secret societies and groups. Thus, at the apex of the New World Order we find Jews: Jewish masters, organizers, planners, and operatives, Gentiles play a lesser, subordinate role.

### *No Honor Among Thieves*

Since human nature is human nature and there is "no honor among thieves," Illuminati groups often vie for superiority. They compete; conflicts occur. There are winners and losers in each stage of human history. Yet, we can best perceive their disputes as, at most, internecine conflict or intra-family war. The Hegelian dialectic is, after all, played out even inside Satan's intimate circle of associates. John Kerry and George W. Bush are both alumni of Skull and Bones; yet their competition for the Presidency was no doubt legitimate. No matter which won the Oval Office, the Illuminati reigned supreme and its agenda continued.

However, at the core of this larger, umbrella family of Illuminati orders and groups is, indeed, a smaller, more shadowy and more secretive inner cabal. This small group of exclusive men is the "world brain," the kabbalistic driver of the global conspiracy. It possesses the power to organize and oversee the many subordinate groups and enforces discipline and order among them. This evil cabal is far superior to the chief executives (Presidents, Prime Ministers) of nations and is, itself, guided, and overseen by the *Hierarchy*, spirit entities from an unseen realm. Christians know this hierarchy as devils, or demons.

## *Do They Use Magic?*

You ask about magic. The Illuminati elite *must* practice magic. Higher-level Illuminati are occult magicians by necessity, because initiates are subservient to these spirit entities in the unseen world. In conducting rituals the elite are honoring and obeying their superiors in both the spiritual hierarchy and the human chain of command. Just as in a great military corps, Illuminist subordinates must continually demonstrate loyalty and discipline. In the military this is demonstrated by an austere regime of otherwise inexplicable rites and ceremonial observances, including salutes exchanged, rank etiquette, flags and unit insignia and myriad other symbols, wearing of uniform items in a prescribed ritualistic manner, and adherence to military regulations and customs. So, too, do the Illuminati adepts signify their fidelity, orderly subservience, and standing in the overall pecking order through symbology, signs, handshakes, coded language, ritual magic, worship, adoration of idols, and other means. Ceremonial law and tradition is strictly enforced within the Illuminati system.

You ask, does ceremonial magic work? Are prescribed rituals efficacious? If you believe, as I do, that powerful and intelligent spiritual entities are behind these practices, then it stands to reason that these entities have the power to "reward" their human disciples, adepts, and chelas (students) in the Illuminati fold.

But magic works in other ways as well. Its knowledge distinguishes the degree or level of superiority attained by an individual. Magic reinforces the initiate's belief system in the goals of the Illuminati. Ritual practices create a smug, interior feeling that the practitioner of magic is special, an insider in an arcane fraternity, and part of a camaraderie of Illumined associates possessing *"secret"* and *"forbidden"* knowledge. Magical work is a multilayered activity with benefits at many levels—material, spiritual, and psychological. Man, even so-called modern, scientific man, is a superstitious creature, and the Illuminati appear to be "true believers" in the efficacy of magic.

### *Performed in Plain Sight*

Ritual magic performed "in plain sight" is an extraordinarily frequent occurrence among the elite. It provides a prime opportunity for the occult illuminatus to pridefully taunt and mock the general public, whom he views as profane and vulgar and deserving of being tricked and deceived. Magical work done openly, but occultly hidden, signals to fellow conspirators the reality that their common, deceptive scheme is succeeding. Again, we find, then, a certain sense of megalomania and arrogance among the elite who perform ritual magic.

Finally, magic is also self-fulfilling. Those who believe in its effectiveness and who exert themselves in its ritualistic exercise will usually *endeavor* to produce the desired effects. A Black Magic—or so-called left-hand magic ritual—say a hex on an enemy, may work simply because those who perform the ritual have the capacity, the capability, and the willful desire to execute real-world acts designed to achieve desirable objectives.

## SEVEN

***Tikkun Olam: When the Jews Ascend the Throne of Absolute Global Dominion...***

# "Will You Walk Into My Parlour?"

*The Spider and the Fly* is a famous poem by Mary Howitt, published in 1829. The first line of the poem is "Will you walk into my parlor? said the Spider to the Fly." The curiously fascinating story tells of a cunning Spider who seeks to ensnare a naïve Fly through the use of seduction and flattery. It is a cautionary tale of evil entities who use charm and smooth talk to disguise their grotesque intentions. Here are the first two stanzas:

"Will you walk into my parlour, said the Spider to the Fly.
Tis the prettiest little parlour that you ever did spy;
The way into my parlour is up a winding stair,
And I've a many curious things to show you when you are there."

"Oh no, no," said the little Fly," to ask me is in vain,
For who goes up your winding stair can ne'er come down again."

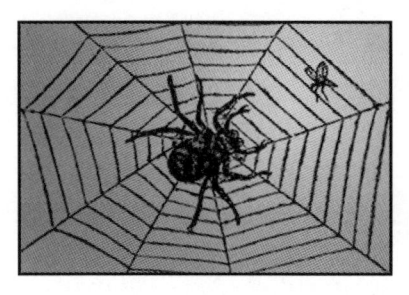

The clever but dangerous Spider reminds me of the seductive "God-talk" of the Jew. "Will you walk into my parlour," he warmly invites the unsuspecting Christian. You will find, he smoothly says, that we Jews are God's Chosen, divine heirs. We promise you *Tikkun Olam*, a "remending" or remaking of the world. It will be a Golden Age of peace and prosperity, a utopia. Come, enter my parlour, up a winding stair...I've a many curious things to show when you are there.

## *A Golden Age for the Jews*

In Rabbi Michael Higger's celebrated 1932 book *The Jewish Utopia*, the "coming world"—a term used in the Jews' Babylonian Talmud—will be a radiant place in which the "righteous" Israel and the Jews will sit atop the heap of nations and peoples. Their Zionist King, the one *The Protocols of the Learned Elders of Zion* refers to as the "King-Despot" and as "The Sovereign Lord of All the World," will usher in a Golden Age for Jews, a Messianic millennium of peace and prosperity. All the world's wealth will be in the hands of the Jews. They shall be a divine race.

Justice will be meted out and all conflicts arbitrated wisely according to Talmudic Law *(Halakah)*, and the Supreme Court of Israel in Jerusalem will be the final arbiter of right and wrong. The world will be reconstructed, mended, and revised *(Tikkun Olam)* according to the pattern outlined in the *Babylonian Talmud*. Judaism will be the supreme religion.

In sum, the Jewish Utopia will be a blissful era of utter contentment, prosperity, and joy—for the Jews. But, what of the Gentiles? What will be their lot once the Messianic Age commences?

The Supreme Court of Israel, architecturally complete with phallic design, a pyramid and obelisk, was built with Rothschild money.

## Gentiles Given an Opportunity

Rabbi Higger, in *The Jewish Utopia*, as well as other authoritative references, makes clear that in the rabbis' ideal world, the inferior Gentiles will be given an opportunity to demonstrate their allegiance to the Judaic deity. They must turn from "idol" worship, including the Christian idolatrous practice of worshipping Jesus. If they do, they will earn the right to be called *"righteous."* If not, then their fate will be that of the *"wicked."* They will be put to death by method of beheading.

Once the "wicked" (i.e. the spiritually dissident Gentiles) are dealt with, then, says Higger, global peace shall ensue.

## Some Will Become Donkeys

Another authoritative Jewish religious leader, the late Sephardic Rabbi Ovadia Yosef, Chief Rabbi in Israel, further elaborated on this topic in a series of radio sermons he gave in 2010. Yosef, spiritual leader of the ultra-conservative Shas political party, a faction which helped Prime Minister Benjamin Netanyahu's rise to power, said that in the coming world, Gentiles may be likened to "donkeys and beasts of burden." The main reason for the very existence of Gentiles, the Rabbi explained is that they are to serve as slaves for the Jews. That, he said, is their "sole purpose."

Quoted in *The Jerusalem Post*, Rabbi Yosef went on to say that, "without this purpose, the non-Jew, the *goy*, has no place in the world. That is why they were created."

The "good news" for Gentiles, according to Yosef, is that because of their value as slaves to Israel, the Gentile servants will be blessed by God with a long life so that their usefulness to Jewish people will be amplified.

Rabbi Yosef compared the life and value of a Gentile to that of a donkey. Each has monetary value but only due to their usefulness in doing labor for their Jewish *effendi* (masters).

Yosef's teachings are supported by the Babylonian Talmud, and even the premier religious colleges in Israel—such as the Talmudic College, Merkaz Hárav, in Jerusalem emphasize that compared to Jews, Gentiles are of a lower spiritual caste, having

Chief Rabbi Ovadia Yosef claimed that according to the Talmud, Gentiles were created only to serve the Jews. He is shown here with Prime Minister Benjamin Netanyahu.

the status of animals rather than humans.

## Gentiles Must Cease Their Idolatrous Worship

If the Illuminati Jews do complete their Great Work and set up a totalitarian New World Order—a future world which many glowingly refer to as the Jewish Utopia—perhaps the Gentile whose status is but that of a slave, or donkey might find himself fortunate. As I've noted, most non-Jews will simply be terminated. Only those fit and able to do manual work for the Jewish effendi are worth keeping, but then only if they renounce their idolatrous worship of this "blasphemer" and "destroyer of Israel." (According to the Jews' Talmud), Jesus Christ.

Thus, we find that in the Jews' religion, Talmudic Judaism, the death of virtually every non-Jew on earth is prescribed. When the Jews establish their "Future World"—their earthly Kingdom of Zion, only those Gentiles who agree to give their wealth to the Jewish masters (the "Effendi") and agree to serve them as animals of burden will be allowed to live.

In the Talmud, the Jews' books of laws and Judaism's most holy book, it is promised that when the Jews receive their kingdom and are redeemed, "it will be a day of light for them." Not so, however for the Gentiles. For them the establishment of the throne of Zion "is darkness and not light." *(Talmud, Sanhedrin 98b, 99a)*.

To emphasize the point, the Talmud brands Jesus Christ a "bastard," a "fornicator," and a "blasphemer." It says that neither he nor the Christians who believe in Him will enter the "future world" when the Jews rule earth *(Sanhedrin 105a)*.

## Gentiles' Property and Women to be Seized

All Gentiles (non-Jews), called "goyim" (cattle), come under scathing attack from the Talmud, which is the principal teaching tool of today's rabbis and the source of their most cherished doctrines, rituals, and religious practices. The Talmud gives the Jews, said to be a divine and holy nation, the right to seize the property of all Gentiles without compensation. It makes the rabbis the chief authority for all the world's population and warns that "whosoever disobeys the rabbis deserves death" *(Erubin 21b).*

### Filthy Gentile Women May be Used for Sex

Gentile women come in for special scalding by the Talmudic rabbis. The Talmud tells male Jews it is their prerogative to use Gentile women for sex without restriction. In any case, "All Gentile women without exception are: Niddah, Shifchah, Goyyah, and Zonah" (menstrual filth, slaves, heathen and prostitutes) *(Sanhedrin 81b and 82a).*

There is a special section in the Talmud setting forth what are called the "Noahide Laws" which govern the religious behavior of Christians in the Jewish–ruled world to come. Because they worship a false god (Jesus) and make him their "idol," they shall be put to death *(Sanhedrin 57a).*

### The Best of the Gentiles—Kill!

In this future world in which Jews shall collectively be their own "Messiah" and a Jewish monarch will rule the nations with harsh methodology, it is proclaimed dangerous for the Jewish *Effendi* (masters) to permit any but the most dumb and servile of Gentiles to live. The others—the ones with intelligence and drive—shall be killed to prevent their spoiling the "perfect world" environment experienced by their wealthy, blessed Jewish masters. Therefore, the Talmud prescribes that, "The best of the Gentiles—kill! The best of snakes—smash its skull" *(Kiddushin 66e).*

For those Gentiles who are allowed to live, things will be bleak. Their Jewish masters will give them sufficient food and shelter so that they remain healthy and have a long life in which to give service to their racial superiors. But as slaves, wholly subject to the desires and whims of the *Effendi,* "non-Jews will be given the place of an ass (donkey) in the future world."

Children born to Gentiles will surely be limited in number, because it is understood that, "a child born to a Gentile is that of a beast" (Mik. Viii and see *The Jewish Encyclopedia*, Funk and Wagnalls Company, Volume 10, p.621).

## Jews Who Convert to Christianity

Jews who dare to cheapen their race and dilute their royal bloodline by converting to Christianity will find that the religious courts to be set up around the world in the Zionist Kingdom will deal with them quite severely. Their betrayal is looked upon both with horror and with boiling fury by the rabbis. In a 1962 edition of the Maimonidean Code (The late Rabbi Maimonides is considered the greatest Jewish sage and Talmudic scholar who ever lived), in its *Book of Knowledge*, published in Jerusalem and now honored as the chief source and guide of the Jewish religion, we find a command to kill all "infidels" who are turncoats: "It is a duty to exterminate them with one's own hands."

This form of Talmud extermination generally means that the person is to be tied or held down and strangled. Alternatively, he or she may be beaten to death by assailant's fists. But the death must be by hand, to emphasize the utter abomination the Jewish "criminal" has committed by converting to the much-hated Christianity.

## No Satan, No Hell—For Jews

Interesting is the fact that many Jews today say that they do not believe either in a hell or a Satan. But, then, we discover that what they really mean is that hell and Satan have no relevance to *them*. The Talmud is soothing and assuring in its promises to the Jews that, as divine beings, none will go to the terrible place called hell where Satan, his devils, and various other forms of satanic entities, salamander spirits, and grotesque creatures dwell and immerse their Gentile prisoners in unimaginable, hellish tortures and deprivations.

### The Lubavitcher and the Hatanya

Israel Shahak, Professor at Hebrew University, an honorable man who became a brave critic of Judaism and its future agenda, (see *Jewish History, Jewish Religion: The Weight of Three Thousand Years*, by Shahak) found the teachings of the rabbis repulsive and evil. He particularly was appalled at the teachings of the Hasidim, a very influential Jewish sect, whose Habbad movement (the Lubavitchers) has over the decades drawn into its web of influence such power-brokers as Presidents Reagan, (G.W.) Bush, and Clinton; California Governor Arnold Schwarzenegger, New York Mayor Bloomberg, and countless other notables.

The Lubavitchers' late "Rebbe," Mendel M. Schneerson, who ran this rich and powerful organization from his New York headquarters, was worshipped and adored as a god-man by his followers. Now, about 15 years after his passing, many of the faithful Hasidic disciples and rabbis, well-known for their black garb, beards, and long hair with curls (the number of curls is dictated, to be in accordance with mystical numerological traditions) reputedly expect him to return any day now. They believe their beloved, "Rebbe" will turn out to be the King Messiah who will sit on the throne and reign over the nations from the Temple Mount in Jerusalem. *(Don't hold your breath, Hasidim!)*

According to Professor Shahak, the fundamental reference book of the Lubavitchers and the Habbad is the celebrated *Hatanya*. There we find the future of the Gentiles all lined up and ready to be implemented. Of course, as does the basic Talmud which the Hasidim adore, the *Hatanya* has much to say about non-Jews. First we find that non-Jews are "totally satanic creatures in whom there is absolutely nothing good. Even a non-Jewish embryo is qualitatively different from a Jewish one."

What's more, "the very existence of a non-Jew is 'inessential,' whereas all creation was created solely for the sake of the Jew."

Shahak notes that, "The book *(Hatanya)* is circulated in

countless editions" and distributed to Jews around the world. "In Israel," says Shahak, "these ideas are widely disseminated among the public at large, in the schools and in the army."

Now we know why the Israeli soldiers are so inhuman, vicious, and brutal in their treatment of the Palestinians. The Palestinians are considered by Jews as worthless beasts, "inessential," and even satanic. How could a righteous divine Jewish soldier possibly permit Satan's own (Gentiles) to be spared. Why not torment him a bit, show him the lash of the conqueror, then put him out of his misery?

## *American Evangelicals Agree*

Evidently this rather barbaric attitude has caught on even in some evangelical Christian circles. At least it seems so from the comments by Trinity Broadcasting Network (the world's largest Christian network with over 1,700 broadcast stations) pastor, San Antonio's John Hagee. Hagee is demanding that the United States, Israel's chief ally in its ongoing war against its Arab and Persian (Gentile) neighbors, take pre-emptive action and go ahead and "nuke" countries like Iran. "God wants it done—use nuclear weapons now and destroy Israel's enemies"—that's the argument Mr. Hagee trumpets from his platform pulpit. And his message must be very popular among evangelicals—his

Pastor John Hagee (left), shown here with friend, Israel advocate Senator John McCain, preaches Jews don't need Jesus for salvation. He is demanding America nuclear bomb Israel's enemies in the Middle East, or else God will punish us.

Cornerstone Church is packed to the rafters with thousands of attendees, cheering and rah-rahing to their Pastor's thundering demands for death to be meted out to Israel's neighbors who are thwarting the redemption of the Jews and putting up obstacles to the glorious Jew-led Millennium Kingdom to come.

Meanwhile, Dr. Samuel Gipp, well-known and highly respected among Independent Baptists, wrote in one of his newsletters that he would cherish the sight of Palestinian youth lying down in the streets and taking a bullet to the head from Israeli soldiers. Gipp's dream for the Palestinians seems at odds with those expressed by Jesus Christ who preached to turn the other cheek, to do unto others as you would do to yourself, and who prophesied that, "the meek shall inherit the earth."

Jesus, in my view—and that of the New Testament, desires that no man perish, but that all receive eternal life and reside with Him in his heavenly abode. Such principles regrettably, do not today find much of an audience, and certainly are not those held by many evangelicals, the majority of whom believe to various degrees in Jewish Supremacism and who actually pray and long for a Jewish Kingdom to quickly come to fruition. The Apostle Paul knew of these types of pseudo-Christians in his day. He called them "Judaizers" and proclaimed their pro-Zionist religious teachings to be accursed witchcraft *(Galatians 1-3)*.

### Shocked When the Rabbinic Police Come For Them

Won't these holier-than-thou Judaizer "Christians" be shocked and dismayed when their esteemed Talmudic rabbis and the Sanhedrin actually do mount the throne of world power and commence to dispense Talmudic justice to Gentiles (including *them*, the Judaizers). They, the Judaizers, will receive all the harsh punishments set forth these many years in advance in the Jews' most holy book, the Talmud.

Perhaps when these Judaizers and their families are taken away to the gulags, they will remember yet another prophecy of

Jesus. Of the Jews and their schemes for global domination and genocide, the Lord Himself warned, *"They will kill you and thinketh they do God service" (John 16:2).*

In fact, the Jews *will* be doing "God" service. That is, in killing "the best of the Gentiles," they will be doing *their* god service. I know *his* despicable name, even if the Judaizers are too spiritually numbed at present to recognize it. His name—the name of the deity honored and worshipped by the Talmudic Jews—is *Lucifer!*

# EIGHT

# The Jewish Antichrist

> "And then shall that Wicked be revealed, whom the Lord shall consume with the spirit of his mouth, and shall destroy with the brightness of his coming…"
> — *II Thessalonians 2:8*

> "I am come in my Father's name, and ye receive me not: if another shall come in his own name, him ye will receive."
> — Jesus Christ
> *John 5:43*

The Jewish rabbis scoff and ridicule the Christian teaching of the Antichrist to come. They say that the passages in the New Testament which point to this evil person, a counterfeit of Christ, emerging to seize the reins of world power as Messiah in the last days is nothing more than popular fiction.

The Jews, however, do posit faith and hope in a future *Jewish Messiah* whom, they say, shall come to lead the Jewish Nation—composed of all the Jews in the world—and insure a radiant, sun-filled New Age of Jewish supremacy and hegemony over planet earth.

The Talmud envisions this future world as a place where the "righteous" (divine Jews) hold all the world's wealth in their hands. There will be a world capital, Jerusalem, and a world Supreme Court, also in Jerusalem.

As the Talmudic rabbis envision things, in the future world, most of the Gentiles, the *goyim* (cattle), will be killed, but a few shall remain, as slaves of the *effendi* (Jewish masters). They must be obedient to the Talmud's Noahide Laws and must renounce Christ or they will be beheaded. This shall be the "Jewish Utopia," and indeed, that is the very title of an insightful book written by prominent Rabbi Michael Higger.

## *Christianity's Antichrist vs the Jewish Messiah to Come*

Is the Christian antichrist and the Jewish Messiah one and the same? Is the sinister and infamous man of sin whom the Christians also call the "Son of Perdition" destined to come from the very bloodline and nation that produced the Saviour of mankind, the Messiah Jesus Christ? Could the one whom the Jews most long for, their great and future king, turn out to be the one whom the Christians loathe and despise, knowing him to be the very antithesis of righteousness, the embodiment of all evil, and the express incarnation of Satan the destroyer?

After many decades of research and investigation in this cardinal area of Bible prophecy and Judaic religious eschatology, (study of future things), I am pleased to submit the more cogent facts I have collected. As the currently popular media slogan goes, "I report, you decide."

## *A Slew of Potential Antichrists*

Before delving into this matter, however, I would like to point out that there are some who are convinced that the Antichrist will not come from Jewish stock but will be a Catholic Pope. Others point to the prophecies of the French mystic, Nostradamus, whose murky and elliptical "Quatrains" spoke of an evil world leader to come on the scene in the last days wearing a "blue turban." A few suggest this blue turban could be the blue beret or helmet of a United Nations military commander.

As this book goes to press, a bestselling author is proposing that the antichrist will be a Moslem. The media's bogeyman, the shadowy Saudi Arabian Osama bin Laden, seems to be the prototype for this theatrical Moslem "antichrist."

Of course, in every historical era, the popular imagination produced an image of the "antichrist," and no surprise, there always seemed to be some real-life candidates for this drama of "pin the tail on the antichrist." In the 30s and 40s, Mussolini and Hitler were likely candidates. In the 50s some suggested the Kremlin monster Stalin as a definite antichrist possibility. Henry Kissinger, the cunning and deceptive 1970s master of diplomacy, was said to embody the traits to be found in the antichrist.

When Gorbachev came on the scene, some imaginative people were aghast at the birthmark on his forehead that was shaped somewhat akin to the map outline of Italy. In a panic, they wanted to know, could he, Mikhail Gorbachev, turn out to be the antichrist and head of a Revived Roman Empire?

## *Bill Clinton's Wolfish Lust and John F. Kennedy's Fatal Wound*

I also recall a few writers who emailed and wrote to me in the 90s about President Bill Clinton. In their minds his magnetic charm and personality, not to mention his wolfish lust and giant ambition, gave Mr. Clinton a leg up in the race for who would be the dreaded antichrist.

One gentleman about 20 years ago sent me a copy of a book he had written in which he claimed that the slain President John F. Kennedy would miraculously be brought back to life. So astonished and awed would be the people of planet earth by this potent supernatural event they would all, *enmasse*, hail the newly resurrected, undeniably charismatic former President of the United States as a Christ figure and crown him with all glory as King of a worldly empire.

## A Sure Word of Prophecy

While I find all such proposals—from Hitler and Stalin to Clinton and a resurrected JFK—slightly amusing and sometimes even provocative, I also know that, on the whole, such enterprising thoughts and suggestions are a monumental waste of time. In fact, the Holy Bible is quite clear in giving us the parameters and description of the man destined to come as the Antichrist, the Son of Perdition. If we study the Word of God, we are not in the dark concerning this great controversy. Through the divine power of our Lord Jesus Christ we are not left in a condition of instability, blind as to what is to come. Instead, we can rely with confidence on what the Apostle Peter called, a "sure word of prophecy."

## The Antichrist Will Come From the Synagogue of Satan

The fact is God has actually named the nation, people, and religious system which has the tragic destiny of being chosen to ravage the world in the last days and produce supreme evil. This monstrous system, the Scriptures say, shall engulf the whole of humanity and the physical earth itself in a sea of blood and terror. Such horror will have never been experienced, from the days of the Mongol hordes of Genghis Khan to the barbarism of Attila the Hun and the Red Terror of Lenin and Stalin.

The Scriptures emphatically direct our focus to the sinister, destructive, *Synagogue of Satan* that will scald and savage the people of God and bring in a flood of bloodshed and blasphemy. The Synagogue of Satan is to be a *global system* (see *Revelation 17* and *18*) in which Judaism and World Jewry (the Jews dispersed in many nations) will participate in accomplishing its Satanic goals. As Jesus warned, their father is the Devil and his works they will do.

Certainly the antichrist will lead the worldwide Synagogue of Satan in its dastardly "Great Work" of destruction and in the setting up of the last days, totalitarian Jewish-ruled kingdom on earth. But while he will undoubtedly be a Jew (or *say* that he is a "Jew"), the antichrist could be the President of the United States, the leader of the European Community, or yes, even a future Catholic Pope. Whatever is his base of power, the Antichrist will covertly be the head of the Synagogue of Satan.

The Bible minces few words in identifying this supreme evil that, in the last days, spreads its parasitic, serpentine coils across the globe, encircling and constricting and squeezing the breath out of every nation on the planet. In *Revelation 2:9* and again in *3:9*, we are directed to the Synagogue of Satan. By the power of this satanic religious system the world shall enter into the "hour of temptation," when every soul shall be tested. He that overcometh shall enter into the kingdom of heaven. All who fail, who take the "mark, or the name, or the number of the beast" (666), shall be thrown into the Lake of Fire. This is the hellish, external and abominable place reserved for the Devil, his angels and his human followers.

### *The Temple of God and Heavenly Jerusalem*

*Revelation 2* and *3* tell us of the "tribulation" and trials the Synagogue of Satan will put Christians through. Many will be thrown into prison. Suffering will be immense. Nevertheless, we are encouraged not to fear any of these things but to be patient and be faithful and God will lift us into victory as overcomers.

> *"Because thou hast kept the word of my patience, I also will keep thee from the hour of temptation that is to come upon all the world, to try them that dwell upon the earth...*
>
> *"Him that overcometh will I make a pillar in the temple of my God, and he shall go no more out: and I will write upon him the name of my God, the name of the city of my God, which is new Jerusalem, which*

*cometh down out of heaven from my God, and I will write upon him my new name."*

We note two important things mentioned in this passage: (1) "The temple of my God," and (2) The "new Jerusalem which cometh down out of heaven." In these two elements we find further answers to our quest for uncovering the national, racial and religious identity of the antichrist.

The prophecies in the book of *Revelation* were given to the Apostle John by Jesus Christ, who is called the very "Spirit of Prophecy." Jesus, in *Revelation 19:10*, promises the saints of God that they will: (1) Be made a "pillar" (of remembrance) in the heavenly Temple of God, and (2) Shall reside forever in the City of God, the New Jerusalem "which cometh down out of heaven."

We find it of the utmost significance that Satan and his wicked people, the Synagogue of Satan, will attempt to produce both a counterfeit "Temple of God" and an earthly "City of Jerusalem," which they will falsely claim to be the Holy City.

While God's Temple and an Holy City are of heavenly origins, those of the Jews will be of *earthly* (or "earthy") origin. Theirs is an earthly religion, that of Christ a heavenly. The difference between earthly and heavenly is monumental. In *I Corinthians 15:47-50* we are told:

> *"The first man is of the earth, earthy: the second man is the Lord from heaven.*
>
> *"As is the earthy, such are they also that are earthy: and as is the heavenly, such are they also that are heavenly.*
>
> *"And as we have borne the image of the earthy, we shall also bear the image of the heavenly.*
>
> *"Now this I say, brethren, that flesh and blood cannot*

*inherit the kingdom of God; neither doth corruption inherit incorruption."*

## The Zionist Plan to Rebuild the "Temple of God"

The scriptures tell us over and over that God does not and will not reside in a Temple built by human hands. He Himself has constructed this great edifice of worship out of "heavenly" (that is, spiritual) materials which surpass anything that natural man could attain (See *Ephesians 2* and *3*).

You will recall from a study of both history and the Holy Bible that the Jews have constantly sought to build a Temple right here on earth where God would reside. Each time it was polluted and defiled by the Jews and made into a place of satanic activity.

Solomon, King of Israel, built such a Temple, but then he disobeyed God by taking foreign women to be wives and concubines, women who turned away the King's heart from the true God and induced him to introduce the worship of false gods. Asherah poles, idols to these false gods, were set up in the Temple. Solomon was apparently deep into sorcery and occultism, and in *I Kings 10:14* we are told that annually the King required the high priests of the defiled Temple to give him in tribute 666 talents of gold. Note that number: *666*, the number of the beast and antichrist *(Revelation 13)*.

Because of his betrayal of God due to his lust and idolatry, King Solomon is honored and revered today, both by Kabbalistic Jews and by the covertly Jewish secret society of Freemasonry.

## Babylon and 666

Modern scholars of Babylon and the Chaldees have discovered that the Babylonians were, as are the Jews of today, practitioners of Gematria, occult numerology, and that the number of the Great Goddess of the Babylonian Empire was "666." She was called the "triple goddess" by virtue of number, representing as she did the trifold nature of the pagan Babylonian Godhead:

Father, Mother and Son.

The Jews of today have as their holy book of laws *(Halakah)* the *Babylonian Talmud,* a satanic book that is chock-full of all manner of obscenities, debauchery, and deception. The contents for this book (actually a set of some 63 books, depending on the edition) came originally out of Babylon, where the Jews were held captive by the monarch and conqueror Nebuchadnezzar and his son, Belshazzar, for many decades during the era of the prophets Jeremiah and Daniel.

The Talmud was at first the "Oral Laws" handed down by the rabbis. Jesus said they were "man-made traditions" and noted that they brought men into bondage to Satan. The high priests of Judaism, however, hold these oral laws, now set forth in writing, in such esteem that the Orthodox rabbis study the Talmud almost to the exclusion of the Torah and Old Testament.

## Ezekiel Sees What is Kept Hidden Behind the Walls by the Learned Elders of Zion

Ezekiel, in the Old Testament, exposed the ritualistic horrors that secretly were observed in the hidden chambers of the Jews' Holy Temple. Ezekiel was taken by God to these hidden chambers where he saw the high priests, the "Learned Elders of Zion," worship the pagans' sun god as well as other satanic, astrological deities. These things were, however, done by the high priests behind closed doors in a vain effort to deceive the people:

> *"Then said he unto me, Son of man, dig now in the wall: and when I had digged in the wall, behold a door.*
>
> *"And he said unto me, Go in, and behold the wicked abominations that they do here.*
>
> *"So I went in and saw; and behold every form of creeping things, and abominable beasts, and all the idols of the house of Israel, pourtrayed upon the wall*

*round about.*

*"And there stood before them seventy men of the ancients of the house of Israel, and in the midst of them stood Jaazaniah the son of Shaphan, with every man his censer in his hand; and a thick cloud of incense went up.*

*"Then said he unto me, Son of man, hast thou seen what the ancients of the house of Israel do in the dark, every man in the chambers of his imagery? for they say, The LORD seeth us not; the LORD hath forsaken the earth.*

*"He said also unto me, Turn thee yet again, and thou shalt see greater abominations that they do.*

*"Then he brought me to the door of the gate of the LORD'S house which was toward the north; and, behold, there sat women weeping for Tammuz.*

*"Then said he unto me, Hast thou seen this, O son of man? turn thee yet again, and thou shalt see greater abominations than these.*

*"And he brought me into the inner court of the LORD'S house, and, behold, at the door of the temple of the LORD, between the porch and the altar, were about five and twenty men, with their backs toward the temple of the LORD, and their faces toward the east; and they worshipped the sun toward the east.*

*"Then he said unto me, Hast thou seen this, O son of man? Is it a light thing to the house of Judah that they commit the abominations which they commit here? for they have filled the land with violence, and have returned to provoke me to anger: and, lo, they put the*

*branch to their nose."*
—*Ezekiel 8:8-17*

This secret worship of Satan, his dark angels, and false gods continues to this day among the "Learned Elders of Zion," and so the discoveries by Ezekiel of what went on behind closed doors remain of great interest to all who seek the truth about the depths of Satan concealed in the Judaic religion of the 21st century.

### *Jesus' Prophecy of the Destruction of the Temple*

In the days of Imperial Rome, in a vain bid to impress the Jews, his royal subjects, King Herod rebuilt a magnificent new Temple in Jerusalem. It was where the Jews, in the days of Jesus, carried out their ritual sacrifices of animals and other practices. But once again, Jesus saw that the Jews were using the Temple for profane and unholy purposes. In righteous indignation he cast the moneychangers out of the Temple, and then he angered the Pharisees by prophesying that the Temple of Herod would be utterly destroyed so that not one stone would be left upon another.

This prophecy astonished even his disciples; nevertheless, in 70 AD, thirty-seven years after Christ's crucifixion and resurrection at age 33, the Roman General Titus, who later became a Caesar, invaded and destroyed the wicked city of Jerusalem. The Temple, too, was destroyed, so that one stone was not left upon another!

The Jews were either killed, were taken captive and became slaves, or fled into other nations and territories where they went into hiding. Thus began the *Diaspora*, the dispersion of the Jews.

### *New King David of the Jews*

Since that momentous time when Titus destroyed their Temple and city, the Jews have schemed and plotted to restore their lost "glory." Continually, the rabbis have preached to their congregations that someday they would return to the so-called Holy City and rebuild their Temple, re-instituting the old sacrifices. No doubt they also relish the thought of once again introducing into the Temple the doctrines and practices of Kabbalah—sorcery, magic, and the worship of polytheistic deities. Among the polytheistic deities worshipped by Jews today is a Supreme Mother (Goddess), the Father God, and their Son and Daughter, as detailed in the Kabbalah.

The Son, whom the Kabbalah teaches was produced by the sexual union of the Supreme Mother and Father, will eventually incarnate in a human body and be crowned as Israel and World Jewry's monarch, the new King David. As such he will preside over both the Jewish Kingdom that will encompass the whole world, its capital being Jerusalem. The Kabbalah teaches that World Jewry, with its new, wise King David on the throne, will be its own, collective Messiah, and the Jews will reign over the Gentile nations as masters and gods. The Kabbalah depicts these holy Jews as the *"Light of the World."* Their illuminations, according to the Kabbalah, come from their Holy Serpent, Leviathan.

Yes, the most holy symbol of the Jewish people, according to the Kabbalah, is the serpent Leviathan.

> This is the symbol of Baphomet, used in witchcraft and in the occult. It is the pentagram star with the head of the goat, representing the carnal nature of man. The hebraic figures encircling the symbol are found in the Kabbalah and spell out "Leviathan." Leviathan is the serpent of the watery abyss, whom the Jews worship. He is literally, Satan, the Devil.

## *The Masonic Mausoleum" and "The Congregation of the Dead"*

Freemasonry, a cult and secret society, based on the teachings and symbols of the Jews' Kabbalah (see Albert Pike, *Morals and Dogma*) is a mirror image of the goddess-based religion of the Jews. It is therefore no accident that the chief authority of the Scottish Rite, the world's largest and most influential Masonic fraternity, is its *"Supreme Mother Council"* which meets behind closed doors at the "House of the Temple," in Washington, D.C. Now this Masonic House of the Temple is designed after the Tomb of King Mausos of ancient Greece, whom the word "Mausoleum" was named after.

In *Proverbs 21:16* of the Old Testament, Israel's King Solomon uses the phrase "congregation of the dead." This term accurately and chillingly describes the Jewish religion and people as the "Congregation of the Dead." And in an amazing parallel we find that the Masonic world headquarters in Washington, D.C., is designed by architect John Pope, as a

The House of the Temple, 13 blocks from the White House, in Washington, DC, is headquarters for the Supreme Mother Council of Scottish Rite Freemasonry.

tomb, or place of the dead. Indeed, in practicing and incorporating the principles and rituals of the Kabbalah, which itself emanates from ancient Babylon, the House of the Temple, the seat of the chieftains of Freemasonry, is verily the meeting place of the "congregation of the dead."

### The Jewish Antichrist Comes to Power

Note that the Masons, a Jewish cult with, however, many Judaized Gentiles on its membership rolls, call their great headquarters the "House of the Temple." It is the House but is not the Temple itself. It merely represents—for the present—on planet earth the restored Temple of the Jews, which is yet to be built in Jerusalem. It is this future Temple where the Jewish antichrist, offspring of the Kabbalah's Jewish Father God and Mother Goddess, whom the prophetic scriptures reveal to be the "Son of Perdition," will in days to come enter and declare himself to be God over all. Here is the Apostle Paul's remarkable prophecy concerning the coming of this Jewish Antichrist *(II Thessalonians 2)*:

> *"Now we beseech you, brethren, by the coming of our Lord Jesus Christ, and by our gathering together unto him,*
>
> *"That ye be not soon shaken in mind, or be troubled, neither by spirit, nor by word, nor by letter as from us, as that the day of Christ is at hand.*
>
> *"Let no man deceive you by any means: for that day shall not come, except there come a falling away first, and that man of sin be revealed, the son of perdition;*
>
> *"Who opposeth and exalteth himself above all that is called God, or that is worshipped; so that he as God sitteth in the temple of God, shewing himself that he is God.*

*"Remember ye not, that, when I was yet with you, I told you these things?*

*"And now ye know what withholdeth that he might be revealed in his time.*

*"For the mystery of iniquity doth already work: only he who now letteth will let, until he be taken out of the way.*

*"And then shall that Wicked be revealed, whom the Lord shall consume with the spirit of his mouth, and shall destroy with the brightness of his coming:*

*"Even him, whose coming is after the working of Satan with all power and signs and lying wonders,*

*"And with all deceivableness of unrighteousness in them that perish; because they received not the love of the truth, that they might be saved.*

*"And for this cause God shall send them strong delusion, that they should believe a lie:*

*"That they all might be damned who believed not the truth, but had pleasure in unrighteousness."*

## The Wailing Wall and the Moslem Mosque in Jerusalem

As I noted, since the destruction of the Temple of Herod in 70 AD, the Jews have plotted and schemed to rebuild that blasphemous place of satanic worship. With the establishment of the earthly nation of Israel in 1948, that nation's leaders have endeavored to dispossess the Palestinians of their land and property. In 1967, the fledgling Jewish nation and its army seized the City of Jerusalem, and so today the rabbis and the Jewish faithful go up on the Temple Mount in that city and imagine they are praying to "God" as they rock, sway and chant at the so-called "Wailing Wall." Even the Judaizer Gentiles, including the modern Popes of Rome and Presidents Clinton, Bush, and Obama of the United States, have done so.

On this same Temple Mount sits Islam's holy place, the impressive, golden-domed Mosque of Omar, the "Dome of the Rock." The imams and grand mufti of the Moslem faith say this is the exact spot where their prophet, Mohammed, ascended bodily to heaven. This great Mosque is superseded only by the city of Mecca in Saudi Arabia in the pantheon of Islamic holy places.

The Jews intend to eventually destroy the Dome of the Rock and rebuild their holy Temple on its ashes. To this end, a number of Jewish groups and organizations are working. They have already made and collected various holy artifacts and implements, including the robes and vestments of the high priests, the menorah, the candlesticks and so forth.

## *Ignorant Evangelical Christians Help Install the Antichrist in Power*

Ignorant of Bible prophecy which warns that the antichrist, the "Man of Sin," (aka the "Son of Perdition") will use this rebuilt temple as a staging ground to broadcast his satanic message to the Jews and then to the world at large, thousands of Christians have foolishly contributed millions of dollars to these Jewish groups and organizations. By their contributions, these confused "Christians" believe that they are hastening the return of Christ. They also are persuaded that they are "blessing the Jews" and that God will generously reward them for having done this.

What a triumph for the Jews and for their Lord, Satan, to convince evangelical Christians to rebuild the unholy Temple. Of course, this is in defiance of Jesus, who prophesied its destruction over three decades in advance and caused it to be destroyed. Nevertheless, Zionist propaganda had convinced these ignorant "Christians" that this sacrilege to assist them is an act of "blessing the Jews." In fact, what they are really doing is funding and sponsoring the coronation and reign of antichrist, a reign, which shall culminate in the cruel and inhumane torture and genocidal massacre of Christians and Gentiles across this planet.

Now the Pope of Rome is also marching lockstep with the deceived, Judaizer evangelicals and with the Talmudic Jews. The late Pope John Paul II got aboard the Zionist 666 train in the waning days of his papacy when he issued an encyclical—an official Vatican pronouncement—that the Jews, having rejected Jesus as Messiah nevertheless will be rewarded by God. Their long wait for a Jewish Messiah, said the Pope, *"is not in vain."*

Thus, the Pontiff reassured the rabbis and the Jewish people that the Messiah they have long awaited surely will come. Since Jesus is despised and long rejected by the Jews, it can only be the Antichrist whom they await—the Christ pretender. Yet the Pope has now joined the Jews in enthusiastically awaiting his arrival. And so the Christian establishment, Catholic mainline and evangelicals, unite in a massive antichrist conspiracy unparalleled in human history.

It is no wonder that *II Thessalonians 2* describes the antichrist as a man of sin who "sitteth in the Temple" and whose coming is "with all power and signs and lying wonders." As for those who fall under the spiritual control of the antichrist who sits pretending to be "God" in this rebuilt Temple of the Jews, the scriptures say they are deceived because of their "unrighteousness," and that they shall ultimately perish, "because they received not the love of the truth, that they might be saved."

> *"And for this cause God shall send them strong delusion that they should believe a lie.*
>
> *"That they might all be damned who believed not the*

*truth, but had pleasure in unrighteousness."*
*— II Thessalonians 2:11-12*

### The Jews Will Accept the Antichrist as Their King and Savior

Bible prophecy clearly pictures the antichrist entering the Temple in Jerusalem and declaring that he is God and above all other gods. The Jews will believe in Him because, having rejected Jesus, they have for two thousand years looked expectantly for their new King David to come and take the Kingdom, and establish the Jews as a divine nation and kingdom ruling over the Gentiles. The Jews view their Christ figure as a man who will administer a world based on the Talmud and organized according to Kabbalistic ritual. He shall be, in their imagination, a materialistic man, showering the Jews with riches and all manner of luxurious and dainty goods. Each Jew will, as they imagine it, reside in a fabulous mansion, attended to by Gentile slaves and laborers.

To the Jews, Jesus was clearly unacceptable as King. He did not fit this mold; He came as a servant, the son of a poor carpenter. He had not a place—not even a foxhole—to lay his head. The humble Jesus rode into the Holy City on a donkey. His disciples were not of the higher wealthy classes. He had no slaves and soldiers or army to take booty. He was raised in Galilee, the "land of the Gentiles." When the Roman Governor Pontius Pilate asked Jesus if he was a king, He answered, "I am," but then added, "My kingdom is not of this world." Pilate found Jesus innocent, but the bloodthirsty Jews cried out, *"crucify him!"*

### The Two Essential Messianic Criteria of the Jews

According to Dr. David Novak, Edgar Bronfman Professor of Modern Judaic Studies at the University of Virginia (see book, *The Jewish Christian Dialogue*, Oxford University Press, 1989), Jesus did not fulfill two essential "Messianic criteria:" (1) He did not restore national sovereignty of the Jewish people in the

> **Getting ready to behead Christians?** In 2011, residents of Tel Aviv, Israel were shocked when protesters brought forward a guillotine and paraded it down the streets. *Revelation 13* says that the beast, 666 will mete out beheading as punishment for those who refuse the mark, name or number of the beast.

land of Israel; and (2) He did not bring about God's Universal Kingdom of justice and peace on earth.

The latter criterion, establishment of a "universal kingdom" on earth, refers to the Jewish quest for total dominion over all the Gentile nations. In such a kingdom, the Jewish Messiah will be an absolute ruler, or dictator over the Gentiles. His kingdom will be a theocracy and the Gentiles will be allowed to survive only if they agree to: (1) Honor the Jewish "God" (actually consisting of a multiplicity of gods and goddesses as described in the books of the Kabbalah); (2) Obey the Noahide Laws of the Talmud, which prohibit idolatry and the worship of other gods—Jesus being one, and (3) Agree to serve the divine Jewish race and nation.

So called "Messianic Jews"—Christians who are of the Jewish race but do not subscribe to the religion of Judaism as taught by the rabbis—are said by Professor Novak to be "apostates" who are excluded from the Jewish community. In effect, they are categorized as "Gentiles" regardless of their race and bloodline.

While at first the Jewish Messiah may pretend to be a staunch supporter and enforcer of Talmudic Judaism and be regarded by the Jews as the new David, a servant and King of Israel, his pathological ego will come rapidly to the fore. Full of Satan, he will enter the rebuilt Temple and declare that he is the one true god and is "above all that is called God" *(II Thessalonians 2:3-4)*. Christians will therefore recognize him as the "Man of Sin," the son of perdition: "The Antichrist."

### *Deception and Delusion: The Jews Will Believe A Lie*

Jesus told the Jews, *"I am come in my Father's name, and ye receive me not: if another shall come in his own name, him ye will receive." (John 5:43)*. He also prophesied of many false Christs to come. "If it were possible," Jesus cautioned, "even the very elect will be deceived."

In summary, the Jews are this very day preparing for the day when the Moslems' Dome of the Rock in Jerusalem is destroyed. That event will energize their plan to rebuild Judaism's dark Temple of doom. When it is completed, the Antichrist, the Man of Sin and Son of Perdition, whom they will believe in because of his lies, signs, and wonders, shall go into its sanctuary and receive the kingdom on earth that Jesus refused. The Jews will surely be delirious with joy, and there will be dancing, feasts, and orgies in the streets. The end of all things will be at hand.

# NINE

**How Many Pastors Know That Jews Do Not Worship the God of the Old Testament?**

# True Beliefs of Judaism—The Phallic Cult of Sex Gods and Goddesses

"Judaism is not based on the Old Testament...Judaism's God is not the God of Israel, but the strange gods and goddesses of the Talmud and Kabbalah."
— Michael Hoffman
*Judaism's Strange Gods*

If I were to today ask 1,000 Christian pastors the *names* of the gods and goddesses worshipped in the religion of the Jews, all 1,000 would no doubt consider me absolutely crazy. Every one of these men think that they know all about Judaism. They just know that Judaism has only *one* God, and He's the God of the Old Testament.

Well, regrettably, every single one of these pastors is *wrong*. At one time, it was probably true that the Jews worshipped one god, the great I AM, the Jehovah of the Old Testament. But that was long ago. Today, the rabbis are so much more advanced, so advanced that one god is not enough.

And as far as the Old Testament goes, it's not taught even one hour in most rabbinical schools and seminaries *(Yeshivas)*. The rabbis say that the Old Testament is a book of "myths and fairy tales," an imaginary book that can only be understood by intelligent rabbis who filter its words through the Kabbalah.

## Babylonian Talmud Studied

The rabbis don't need the Old Testament because they have something they think is far better. They have the *Babylonian Talmud*. Yes, the Talmud is where they find their 613 laws and commentary on each. The Talmud is many volumes in length, and Orthodox Jews are judged on how well they know and apply this massive series of books, books that, by the way, are written by ancient rabbis. The Talmud is called the *Babylonian Talmud* because that is where it was begun, when the rabbis and

Ruth Bader Ginsburg, Justice of the Supreme Court of the United States. Ginsburg often quotes from the Talmud in her decisions on the Court. As of 2015, four of the nine justices on the Supreme Court were Jews and a fifth, Antonin Scalia, says he is proud to be called a "Gentile Jew." Scalia also quoted from the Talmud in his decisions and prefers law clerks who are Jewish. He and Ginsburg were close friends who would go on vacation together each year with their spouses.

Jewish layman were hostages to their Babylonian captors, during the era of Jeremiah and Daniel, the prophets.

Now the Talmud, notes Ruth Bader Ginsburg, U.S. Supreme Court Justice, is the Jews' *"guide for daily living."* Without the Talmud, there would be no Judaism. The Talmud says that the wisest rabbis are superior to God in spiritual knowledge and understanding. When God needs advice, the Talmud claims, He goes to the rabbis, who instruct Him. Someday, the Jews will just do away with "God" and assume their destined role as their own Messiah and God.

The Talmud is linked in with the Kabbalah, more books for the Jews, books that further guide the Judaic religion. The Kabbalah is especially useful because it is where a Jew discovers the pantheon of deities found in the religion of Judaism.

### *Popular Delusions About Judaism*

Israel Shahak, famed Professor of Hebrew University in Israel, was one of the foremost authorities in the world on the religion of Judaism. He authored many books on Judaism, including the authoritative, *Jewish History, Jewish Religion: The Weight of Three Thousand Years*, and *Jewish Fundamentalism in Israel*. Although Shahak passed away in 2001, his works continue to educate and direct our attention.

What did Professor Israel Shahak have to say about Judaism?

Shahak notes that Christians are ignorant about Judaism because they hold to what he termed certain "popular delusions":

> "The most important of these popular delusions is that the Jewish religion is, and always was, monotheistic (worshipped just one God)...This historical view is quite wrong." (*Jewish History, Jewish Religion*, 1994, p. 32).

> "The real doctrines dominant in present-day Orthodox

Judaism," Shahak informs his readers, *"has been for the last few hundred years far from pure monotheism."*

> "The decay of monotheism came about through the spread of Jewish mysticism (the cabala, or Kabbalah) which developed in the 12th and 13th centuries, and by the late 16th century had won an almost complete victory in virtually all the centers of Judaism...in latter day Jewish Orthodoxy, especially among the rabbis, the influence of the Cabala has remained predominant."
> —*Jewish History, Jewish Religion*, 1994, p. 32)

## True Beliefs of Judaism

Anyone truly interested in the religion of Judaism must, emphasizes Dr. Shahak, have knowledge and understanding of the *"true beliefs of Judaism."* These ideas are extremely important because they form a key part of the *"explicit system of beliefs"* of today's rabbis and of Zionist politicians and leaders.

So, throw away everything you *thought* you knew about Judaism, including your comfortable—but very antiquated—understanding of the Old Testament. You may, indeed, understand and know of the Jehovah of the Old Testament. *You* may have been instructed in Sunday school and in church by men who *thought* they knew all about Judaism and its God. But, in fact, the Jews almost universally believe in a religion and worship deities whom few Christians know anything at all about.

It is a truth that the so-called "Messianic (Christian) Jews" are the most ignorant of all, though some would argue that this dubious award goes to Christian seminaries and Bible colleges. The Messianic Jews are usually the ones most easily deceived, though they foolishly pretend to be knowledgeable and well-informed.

### Here is Authentic, Not Imagined Judaism

We begin our study of *Judaism* with its understanding of "God." God, to the Jew has no name nor personality. His title is even spelled "G-D." He's a dim and distant "First Cause." He rules no-one but has created many other deities, who are sexual in nature and who rule various aspects of the universe and mankind.

Like the Roman, Greek, Babylonian, and Egyptian deities upon whom this polytheistic and cabalistic system is modeled, Judaism has many gods and goddesses. The various deities constantly have sex with each other. Judaism is, at its foundation, a phallic sex religion.

Even Satan is a god and must be obeyed, or at least propitiated or "bought off" in some way. Many Jews pray to both their version of God and to Satan.

Here is how Dr. Israel Shahak describes this strange and complex system of deities:

> "From the First Cause, first a male god (emerged) called 'Wisdom' or 'Father' and then a female goddess called 'Knowledge' or 'Mother' were emanated or born. From the marriage of these two, a pair of younger gods were born: Son, also called by many other names...and Daughter, also called 'Lady' (or 'Matronist,') a word derived from Latin, Shekhinah, Queen, and so forth.
>
> "These two younger gods should be (sexually) united but their union is prevented by the machinations of Satan, who, in this System, is a very important personage...indeed, Satan has come close to the divine Daughter and even raped her.
>
> "The creation of the Jewish people (a divine race) was undertaken in order to mend the break caused

by Adam and Eve, and…for a moment this was achieved. The male god, Son, incarnated in Moses, was (sexually) united with the goddess, Shekhinah… Similarly, each incident of biblical Jewish history is believed to be associated with the union or disunion of the divine pair…

"Daughter falls closely into the power of Satan (during disunion with Son), while Son takes various female satanic personages to his bed, instead of his proper wife.

"The duty of pious Jews is to restore through their prayers and religious acts the perfect divine unity in the form of sexual union between the male and female deities. Thus, before most ritual acts, which every devout Jew has to perform many times each day, the following cabalistic formula is recited: 'For the sake of the (sexual) congress of the Holy Blessed One (Son) and His Shekhinah…

"Other prayers or religious acts are designed to deceive certain angels…or to propitiate Satan…

"Both before and after a meal, a pious Jew ritually washes his hands, uttering a special blessing. On one of these special occasions, he is worshipping God by promoting the divine (sexual) union of Daughter and Son, but on the other he is worshipping Satan, who likes Jewish prayers and ritual so much that…it keeps him busy for awhile and he forgets to pester the divine Daughter (for sex)…

"For example, the most sacred Jewish formula, 'Hear O Israel, the Lord is our God, the Lord is one,' recited several times each day by every pious Jew,

> Professor Israel Shahak, at his desk in Hebrew University, wrote that in Judaism, many worshippers pray to Satan. He further explained that Judaism is not monotheistic, that there are many gods and goddesses in Judaism.

mean two different things, that the Lord is indeed 'one' but it can also mean that a certain state (of sexual intercourse) in the union of the male and the female deities has been reached or is being promoted by the proper recitation of the formula."

In Judaism, as you can see, sexual activity is everything, and a married couple are judged on how often they can encourage the divine couple—the God and Goddess—to copulate. The idea being that as long as the two (Daughter and Son) are engaging in their incestuous act, the Devil cannot pester the Daughter for more sex.

### *Talmudic Practices Kept Hidden From Christians*

Obviously, this idea and practice of frequent sexual prayers and rituals would be considered as crazy and offbeat by traditional Christians; and that is why the Talmud is never discussed with Christians. Jews are taught to deceive and lie about its true meaning. As Shahak remarks:

"There is yet another misconception about Judaism which is particularly common among Christians... This is the misleading idea that Judaism is a 'biblical religion:' that the Old Testament has in Judaism the central place and legal authority which the Bible has for Christianity... This is far from being the case."

Shahak and other Judaic authorities are very open in their revealing descriptions of the Jewish religion. But their books, other writings, and sermons are reserved for Jews and are rarely read by Christians. So the truth about the sexual depravity and multiple deities in Judaism carefully are kept from view.

### *Christianity is Built on Jesus, and Not on the Teachings and Traditions of the Rabbinical Elders*

The average Christian *assumes* that the Jews are merely Old Testament believers who simply need Jesus to be "completed." Judaism is, in reality, a wicked, corrupt religion of hatred, deception and of deviant, rampant, sexuality and hedonism. There can be no such thing as *"Judeo-Christianity."* The two religions, Judaism and Christianity, are miles apart. Jesus cannot be built *atop* the wicked foundation of Judaism. Jesus *is* the foundation and no other foundation can a man lay.

# TEN

**The Hidden Conspiracy of the Pope, the Vatican, the Jesuits, and the Zionist Elite For a New World Order and the End of All Things**

# Solving the Mystery of Babylon the Great

> "And upon her forehead was written MYSTERY, BABYLON THE GREAT, THE MOTHER OF HARLOTS AND ABOMINATIONS OF THE EARTH."
> — *Revelation 17:5*

In its capacity to fill one's heart with horror and wonder, it is clearly the most staggering prophetic image one can find in the entire Holy Bible. It is recorded in the seventeenth chapter of the book of *Revelation*—John's description of the Whore of Babylon.

The Apostle John saw many terrible things that day on Patmos, the Greek isle to which he had been banished. But perhaps few could compare with this, his vision of the alluring and tantalizing, yet deadly *"Mother of Harlots and Abominations of the Earth."* Who can imagine what breathtaking thoughts raced through John's mind. We do get a glimpse into the Apostle's thought process when we read his words:

> *"And I saw the woman drunken with the blood of the saints, and with the blood of the martyrs of Jesus: and when I saw her, I wondered with great admiration."*
> *—Revelation 17:6*

If there ever was a conspiracy against nations and people of earth this is its highest ensign. The Mother of Harlots, sitting upon a beast, is wealthy beyond compare—she is "decked with gold and precious stones and pearls," and she holds a "golden cup in her hand full of abominations and filth of her fornication." The mysterious woman, regally arrayed in purple and scarlet colour, is drunk, but not from alcohol and strong drink; the Mother of Harlots is drunken "with the blood of the saints and the blood of the martyrs of Jesus." No black widow could compare with this sinister and evil woman. This is no lady. This is a stone-cold serial killer who feasts on the blood of the saints of Jesus and no doubt leaves the world littered with the remains of destroyed souls.

John had seen many terrible things in his life—and now he was a ripe-old 95 years in age—but this was perhaps the most monstrous of all. So incredible was this sight that John was led to admit, *"I wondered with great admiration."*

Certainly this was a begrudging "admiration," but as they say, give even the Devil his due! Mystery Babylon the Great is a religious system to encompass all the "inhabitants of the earth." Indeed, John was told that the wicked woman reigns over "peoples, and multitudes, and nations, and tongues (languages)."

More than that, the sinful Mother of Harlots sits upon the beast that came up out of the bottomless pit (hell) and will in due time "go into perdition." Yes, the Great Harlot exercises all the ominous and savage power of the horrific beast, which shall bring such utter misery to every man, woman, and child on this planet.

Three important questions haunt our senses and must be answered:

- *Who* is the marvelous, but terrible, woman described as "the Mother of Harlots and Abominations of the Earth on whose forehead is written, "MYSTERY, BABYLON THE GREAT?"

- *Who* is the beast that she sits upon?

- *What* is their terrible plan that is even now quickly coming to pass and that will bring such blood and horror into all our lives?

## *Is This the Pope and the Catholic Church?*

As a young man, I listened to many preachers and Bible prophecy teachers who warned that Mystery Babylon is none other than the Pope and the Roman Catholic Church. From the days of Martin Luther, whose heroism and devotion inspired the Protestant movement and the Reformation, Christian leaders have pointed to Rome as the center of global wickedness in the last days. Many believed that the Pope is the very antichrist, the man of sin whose number is 666.

However, in the span of just one generation—in my lifetime—the ecumenical movement and the tendency of the Christian establishment to grow jaded and lukewarm have significantly cooled the ardor of Pastors and prophecy teachers. No longer do these men criticize the false teachings and abominations of the Papacy. Instead, they have jumped into bed with the Pope and swallowed the toxins and poisons emanating from the fountain of St. Peter's Basilica in the Vatican.

But the "Falling Away" of the apostate Christian Church

does not change the prophetic truths of the Holy Bible. The question still arises in the hearts of the faithful saints: Is the Vatican and the Papacy "MYSTERY, BABYLON THE GREAT?" Regardless of what our dulled clergy and compromised Church leaders suggest, what does *God's Word* reveal to us?

## *What About the Synagogue of Satan?*

While questions must be answered about the Pope and his Romish Church, there has arisen yet another great competitor for the infamous title of MYSTERY, BABYLON THE GREAT. I refer, of course, to the *Synagogue of Satan (Revelation 2:9 and 3:9)*. In our century, the monolithic power of World Jewry has galloped to the forefront. With its vaults of banks bulging with stolen cash, its balance sheet hefty with plundered wealth, its Israeli nation aided and abetted by the military muscle and diplomatic might of the world's greatest superpower, the Jewish-ruled United States of America, the Synagogue of Satan today sits at the pinnacle of earthly dominion. The Zionist elite have a heinous Plan that is now being worked to usher in the Jewish Utopia. Their Messiah, the Antichrist, will be at its helm. And once this Plan is realized, Gentiles everywhere will tremble with fear and trepidation. Make no mistake about that.

So, which satanic cult will turn out to be MYSTERY, BABYLON THE GREAT? Will it be Rome, or will it be the Jerusalem/Washington, DC axis that makes war on the saints and spills their blood and places all of humankind into the iron jaws of a global, Big Brother Police State? *What does the Bible say?*

## *Solving the Mystery of Babylon the Great*

I am pleased on my *powerofprophecy.com* website to offer you an eye-opening new book. I believe this book will answer many of your questions on this vital, prophetic issue. Frankly there has never been a book exactly like this, authored by a born again Christian of such sterling credentials.

The title of the book: *Solving the Mystery of Babylon the Great*. It was my privilege to author the Foreword. The author is Edward Hendrie. Now I have had a number of fascinating private discussions with Mr. Hendrie, and I have discerned the genuine heart this godly researcher has for Bible truth. His new book is large format and well over 300 pages. What he reveals in these pages is a great *discovery* that God also put in my heart some years ago. Its stunning conclusion will, I promise you, unshackle your senses and enlighten you in a most important way.

### The Zionists and the Vatican Conspiring Together

Hendrie presents a mountain of evidence, buttressed by factual documentation, proving that MYSTERY, BABYLON THE GREAT is *both* of Zionism and of Rome.

The evidence, says Hendrie, leads to the inevitable conclusion "that the Roman Catholic Church was established by crypto

Pope Francis visits the Synagogue in Rome, Italy, in 2016, where he told the assemblage that Jews do not need Jesus, they have their own covenant. The Pope has directed the Catholic Church to cease evangelization of Jews.

Jews as a false 'Christian' front for a Judaic/Babylonian religion." Moreover, "that religion is the nucleus of a world conspiracy against man and God."

Could this be? Could the Vatican and its Supreme Pontiff be the world's greatest and most stultifying evil hoax? Are the sinister leaders of the serpentine Synagogue of Satan the actual hidden masters who pull the strings of the Papacy?

In these momentous days in which Satan is preparing America and the world for the final, gargantuan assault on our liberties, our freedoms, and our very souls, are the Zionist Illuminati elite and the black and scarlet-robed men of Rome conspiring together for our demise?

### *Hendrie An Ex-Catholic and An Attorney*

Who is Edward Hendrie and what qualifies him to write this amazing book? Hendrie is a successful attorney, a constitutional expert. He is author of three other books. To those who may accuse him of being a Catholic basher, let me add that Hendrie is himself an ex-Catholic. Raised in the Catholic faith by devout Catholic parents, he exclusively attended Catholic schools and graduated from America's most prestigious Roman Catholic University—The University of Notre Dame. He subsequently earned his law degree from a Jesuit institution—the University of Detroit, in Michigan.

Imagine: A book like this unmasking Rome, the Jesuits, and the Papacy in a spectacular way, written not by a Protestant with an axe to grind, but by a brilliant man whose entire life was once wrapped around the false claims of Rome and the Jesuit Order—until, the day he met Jesus.

### *The Beast Rises Up in Jerusalem*

That the last days restored nation of Israel will also incorporate within its occult framework the evil organization of Rome is not surprising. As the "Mother of Harlots," she has many "daughters," of which the Catholic Church is one.

*Revelation 9* and *12* tells us the Beast will rise up out of the bottomless pit. *Revelation 12* specifically states this will be Jerusalem, that "great city wherein our Lord was crucified." So we see, then, that Jerusalem, spiritually called "Sodom and Egypt" in *Revelation 12,* will be at the forefront of earthly wickedness in the last days.

ELEVEN

**The Jews Will Take the One Billion Catholics and Millions of Evangelicals Away Beyond Babylon**

# Beyond Babylon

"And I will carry you away beyond Babylon."
— *Acts 7:43*

Throughout the history of the Catholic Church, from its inception in the days of Roman Emperor Constantine until today, Jews have been instrumental in its organization and development. Peter, Paul, Jude, and the other disciples constantly were forced to make war against Jewish infiltrators. Paul, in his letter to the Galatians, warned Christians to not be brought into bondage by falling back into the Jewish traditions and the law! In other letters Paul spoke of the dangers of "Jewish fables" and "Old Wives Tales." He called those who attempted to tilt the Church toward Judaism, "Judaizers" and said they were "accursed" by God.

### Beware the Crypto-Jews

Jewish rabbis and zealots have never ceased from their attempts to

Ignatius Loyola was a military general and a converted Marrano Jew who persecuted those who would not bow to the Pope of Rome. Here he is shown giving Masonic hand signs and dressed in military regalia.

infiltrate and Judaize the Church. As crypto-Jews, many have pretended to be Gentiles and as such, they have been able to become priests and have exercised great authority within the Catholic hierarchy. Sometimes this authority has conferred on Jewish rabbis the power to torture and kill true Christians who oppose the Vatican. Spain's bloody Jew, Torquemada, papal assassin responsible for the millions who perished during the Spanish Inquisition, is one example. The Catholic Counter Reformation, led by a Spanish General, the Jew, Ignatius Loyola, is another.

Loyola was born to a wealthy Jewish Marrano family in 1491. When the King and Queen of Spain announced an edict in 1492 that all Jews who would not convert to Christianity be expelled, Loyola's father reluctantly converted, but like most other Marranos, he and his family were Catholic in name only. John Torrell, founder of the European-American Evangelistic Association, in an exhaustive review of crypto-Jews, writes of the Spanish Marrano Jews:

> "The Illuminati order was not invented by Adam Weishaupt, but rather renewed and reformed. The first known Illuminati order was founded in 1492 by Spanish Jews, called "Marranos," who were also known as "crypto-Jews…hundreds of thousands of Jews had been forced to convert to the faith of the Roman Catholic Church. Publicly they were now Roman Catholics, but secretly they practiced Judaism…
>
> "The Marranos were able to teach their children secretly about Judaism, but in particular the Talmud and the Cabala, and this huge group of Jews has survived to this very day. After 1540 many Marrano's opted to flee to England, Holland, France, the Ottoman empire (Turkey), Brazil and other places in South and Central America. The Marranos kept strong family ties and they became very wealthy and influential in the nations where they lived. But as is the custom with all Jewish people, it did not matter in what nation they lived, their loyalty

was to themselves and Judaism."

San Ignacio De Loyola, then, led a Jewish Illuminati sect that was a precursor to Weishaupt's group that was established some 250 years later. Loyola's cunning and ambition catapulted him to favor, and moving to Rome with the enthusiastic approval of the Pope, he founded the bloody and conspiratorial *Jesuit Order* in 1539.

Adam Weishaupt, founder of the Order of the Illuminati (1776) was a Jew whose Jewish father had supposedly converted to Christianity. Weishaupt became a Jesuit priest and a professor at a Catholic Jesuit University in Bavaria. Funded by Rothschild, Weishaupt's Illuminati secret society infiltrated and took over the leadership of Masonic Lodges and then instigated the French Revolution. The result was tumult, chaos, and the murder of millions of innocents, mostly Christians.

## *Three Jews Masquerading as Christians*

Imagine, between these three Jews masquerading as faithful Catholics—Torquemada, Loyola, and Weishaupt—up to 25 million people lost their lives. We could perhaps also bring up the matter of crypto-Jews Lenin, Trotsky, and their Jewish Communist comrades butchering some 66 million innocents, but I'll save that for another book. For now, we're looking only at satanic Jews wearing the masks of Christendom.

Men like Torquemada, Loyola, and Weishaupt pretended to be Christians and Catholics but each was at least nominally a subordinate of the Pope, the formal head of the worldwide Catholic Church organization. However, it has always been the cherished goal of the Jewish leadership to actually put one of its own directly on the papal throne. What a coup that would be, to have an unrepentant, Zionist zealot Jew fulfilling the role of the Vicar of Christ, infallible leader of tens of thousands of priests, bishops, and cardinals, over one billion laymen, and possessor of untold billions of dollars in cash assets and property belonging

Adam Weishaupt founded the Order of the Illuminati in Bavaria on May 1, 1776, the same year America declared its independence from Great Britain. The all-seeing eye and pyramid on the U.S. one dollar bill is designed based on concepts of Weishaupt's secret order.

to the Catholic Church under its signature and control.

"Generation after generation," reports Edward Hendrie in *Solving the Mystery of Babylon the Great*, "many crypto-Jewish families gained great influence within the Roman Catholic Church to steer its doctrines and policies." The fact that both the Jewish religion and that of Roman Catholicism were based on Babylonian principles made this infiltration so much easier. Essentially, the only thing the crypto-Jews had to do was to identify the few, actual "Christian" characteristics remaining in the Catholic dogma. These focused on the nature of Jesus Christ—his deity and character—and on the essence of the Gospel of the Kingdom. Once "adjustments" and "compromises" could be made in these areas, then the Catholics would be propagandized on the racial and spiritual superiority of the Jews and the entire Vatican operation would be swallowed up.

It might still portray itself as a "Christian Church," but it would actually serve as another worldwide Zionist front. Gentile

Catholics would then faithfully serve the Jews and their King (the Antichrist) erroneously believing they were doing God service. In his epic volume, *The Plot Against the Church*, Maurice Pinay, a loyal Catholic, comments on this "fifth column" infiltration by Jews masquerading as Christians:

> "This 'Fifth Column' is formed by the descendants of the Jews who in early centuries were converted to Christianity...while in secret they carried out clandestinely the Jewish rites and ceremonies...they organized secret synagogues...These apparent Christians but secret Jews...sowed false doctrines... introducing crypto-Jewish Christians into the seminaries...and then into dissident churches."

### *The Jewish Origins of Pope John Paul II*

In 1978 this seemingly impossible goal was realized when a Polish Jew whom the Jewish elite had long mentored and sponsored was elected Pope of Rome. Karol Wojtyla was his Polish name, and he was the son of Emily Katz, a Jew, and Karol Wojtyla, Sr., a retired military officer.

According to official biographers, the Wojtylas rented an apartment from a Jewish landlord. They and their family were relatively prosperous—the young man, Karol, Jr., had a sister who received an advanced degree and become a medical doctor, a profession to which many Jews gravitated.

One of young Karol's lifelong friends, a Jew named Jerzy Kluger, lived in the same town, Wadowice, about 35 miles southwest of Krakow, Poland. As boys Karol and Jerzy did everything together. Karol even played on soccer teams made up of all Jews (except, supposedly, for him), which competed against all-Gentile soccer squads.

On many evenings, the Wojtyla family, including young Karol, were entertained at the luxurious home of the Klugers. They would drink tea, consume Jewish delicacies, and a live musical string quartet performed for them.

It goes without saying that in the 1930s when all this occurred, Jewish communities regularly excluded inferior Gentiles, whom the rabbis taught were unclean and no better than ignorant animals. Jewish boys on athletic teams would never have allowed a Gentile boy to be on their team. Their bigoted parents would never permit such fraternization.

Biographers have no explanation for these significant gaps in explanation, nor do they discuss the fact that to Jews, racial status is determined from the mother's genealogy, not the fathers. Therefore, from inception in the womb of Jewess Emily Katz, to his death of natural causes in April 2005, Karol Wojtyla was a Jew.

It is claimed that as a young man, fearing the Nazis would kill him or possibly take him away to a concentration camp, Karol Wojtyla sought and was given asylum in 1944 in the house of the Archbishop of Krakow. But why would an ethnic Pole, a Gentile, feel himself in danger in the waning days of the war.

Supposedly, prior to 1944, the young Wojtyla escaped Nazi deportation first as a common laborer in a rock quarry and then as a worker at a chemical plant. Is it not likely that the young Jew simply wanted to establish "credentials" as a faithful Catholic.

It is much more likely that as Jews, the affluent Wojtyla family had made a bogus "conversion" to Christianity. When his Jewish genealogy became vulnerable to discovery by the Nazis who occupied Poland, later in the war young Karol Wojtyla—and perhaps other members of the family—made a cash bargain with the Catholic diocese at Krakow. For a price, Wojtyla was allowed to live and hide in the house of the Archbishop of Krakow. Obviously, young Karol Wojtyla was an "important" person whose family wealth and status shielded him. But how many *poor* Jews were allowed this great privilege of sanctuary by the top Catholic prelate in all of Poland?

Biographers say that the young man had begun to study for the priesthood only in 1943. Inexplicably after the war, young Wojtyla chose to became a professional actor and playwright and delayed his priestly studies for several years. His training as an actor in live stage performances was to serve him well as a priest chosen by his mentors early on for high office in the Catholic hierarchy.

### *Pope John Paul II's Hidden Bloodline*

In 2006, my own findings as to Pope John Paul II's hidden Jewish ethnicity were corroborated by—of all things—a well known researcher in Jewish history and religion. Yaakov Wise stated that, absolutely, the late Pope John Paul II's mother, grandmother, and great grandmother were Jewish. Wise found that the surname of the Pope's mother, Emily, was Kaczorowski, or in English, Katz. Indeed, this is a common Jewish surname.

Because he was a Jew, Karol Wojtyla, later to become Pope John Paul II, had to go into hiding during the Nazi era. After the war, he failed to advance as a stage actor and playwright, and entered training for the Catholic priesthood. Seemingly favored by the Catholic hierarchy, the priest Karol Wojtyla advanced swiftly. He was allowed to widely travel at a time when most Poles were refused passports by the Communist government. In 1978 he was elected Pope. The world was shocked that a Pole could be elevated to the papacy, but insiders were not surprised.

The Jewish media gave a lot of coverage to Yaakov's findings. Some commented that the Pope's Jewishness led him to have an "affinity" with the Jews and with Judaism.

My own research and investigation into Pope John Paul II's Jewish roots and into the fictitious legend of his childhood, training, and career so carefully crafted by later biographers, encouraged me to expose the Pope as a Christian imposter and Jewish infiltrator. I warned many times over the years that this Pope was not even a Catholic, let alone a Christian. Indeed, I personally produced and distributed several videos unmasking

John Paul II, including *Is the Pope Catholic?; Lumen 2000;* and *Tower of Infamy.*

As a Protestant, I was surprised to receive, in response to my writings and video documentaries, many hundreds of letters and emails from loyal traditional Catholics who agreed with me and appreciated my revelations. Many expressed their horror at the satanic changes wrought in their Church since the "innovations" of Vatican II were introduced. They especially were horrified about Pope John Paul II's betrayal of what they believed to be the "historic Catholic faith." Some minced no words—"Pope John Paul II is an anti-Pope, a deceiver."

A few went further: "Pope John Paul II is the antichrist," they charged.

The evidence of Pope John Paul II's Jewish ethnicity was, from the beginning, carefully covered up and kept from the Catholic faithful. In this way, the Pope could proceed to radically implement the new, pro-Zionist and anti-Christian doctrines and practices without unduly alarming the Catholic majority who would otherwise be suspicious of what a Jew might do as Pope.

Vladimir Lenin and Leon Trotsky (*nee* Lev Bronstein) carried out a similar subterfuge as Communist leaders in Russia. Following the Bolshevik victory, everywhere, Jews catapulted to places of power. Gentiles were expelled and many killed. The first order of business by the Leninists was a law passed by the rubber stamp, new Jewish-ruled parliament, the Duma, declaring the "crime" of anti-Semitism an offense punishable by death. The masses were none the wiser, erroneously being led to believe that Lenin and the other top-ranked Bolsheviks were patriotic, ethnic Russians. Anyone who dared to publicly "out" those who ran the government as "Jews" were arrested and never heard from again.

### *Into the Abyss of Talmudic Judaism*

In the case of Pope John Paul II, the Catholic faithful were led to believe he was a patriotic Pole. The fact that he was a Polish Jew never entered their minds. The world's press and media dutifully helped carry out this charade. Thus, when John Paul II came out with his "novel" new teachings regarding the Jews and Judaism, teachings diametrically opposed to those of not only Jesus and the Apostles but of previous Popes as well, which horribly mangled the Bible's clear instructions and served to destroy faith in God's Word and reorient the Catholic Church toward a bastardized form of unorthodox, Judaic Christianity, most Catholics believed their Pope was simply being tolerant, liberal, magnanimous, generous to the Jews. They had no idea of the dark agenda that underlay these dramatic changes in doctrine. How could they have known that their new Pope was *not* a Catholic and would sweep the Vatican and the entire Christian establishment into the abyss of Talmudic Judaism?

Unbeknownst to the person in the pew, the Pope had become chief helper to the Jews' Sanhedrin, and the Catholic Church was soon to be cleansed of all remaining vestiges of godliness. In sum, the agenda called for Christianity to become a mere denomination, or sect, of the Judaic religion, itself based on

Pope John Paul II (right) was a crypto-Jew. He made Cardinal Ratzinger (left) head of doctrine for the Vatican. Upon his death, Ratzinger was elevated to the position of Pope Benedict. Both Popes taught that the Jews are "elder brothers" in the faith and do not need Jesus. This insane teaching was in defiance of what the early apostles and Jesus preached.

Babylonian principles. And eventually, it is to be cleansed of Jesus Christ himself.

Upon his ascension to the Papacy, the first visitor invited to his apartment in the Vatican to meet the newly elected Pontiff, Pope John Paul II, was none other than that boyhood friend, the wealthy Jew, Jerzy Kluger. Kluger was even asked by Pope John Paul II to be an emissary for him to the Jewish community, and the Jewish businessman agreed. Approached by news reporters after his visit to the Pope's dwelling, Kluger stated, "the people in the Vatican do not know Jews, and previous Popes did not know Jews, but this Pope is a friend of the Jewish people because he does know Jewish people."

### *Jews Can Disregard Jesus, Says the Pope*

The new Pope John Paul II, once in office immediately began to thaw once icy Vatican-Jewish relations. Choosing as his vehicle the ecumenical papal bull *Nostra Aetate* (Latin, meaning *"In Our Time"*) issued in 1965 by Pope Paul VI, John Paul added to the bull with his own innovative theology. Over the years, the Pope let the Jews know that the old Catholic Church was a relic of yesteryear. The New Catholic Church, John Paul II assured the Jews, included the Jews as Christianity's *"elder brothers."* Jews no longer would be proselytized and evangelized. The Old Covenant of the Jews would be honored and considered still in effect. The Jews, according to the Pope, could reject or ignore Christ and the New Testament without a care or worry.

Pope John Paul II publicly apologized to Jews for wrongdoings against them throughout history by those whom he deemed to be cruel and vicious Christian anti-Semites. The Pope also published a book apologizing for the holocaust. Never did the Pope suggest the Jews offer an apology of their own for their role in crucifying Jesus Christ, for stirring up the Roman Caesars to massacre millions of Christians in the early era of the Christian Church, for their abduction and sacrifice of young

Gentile boys at Passover over the centuries, or for the savage language directed against Jesus and Christians in their holy books, the Talmud and the Kabbalah. It was as if the Christians had perpetually been a conniving, lying, murderous pack of monsters while the Jews were deemed virtuous Saints continuously being persecuted by the devil-obeying Christians.

Strange this was indeed, for the Apostle Paul had reliably reported the many atrocities committed by Jews against Christians and, in *Galatians 4*, he stated that it was the case that those of the flesh (the Jews) who belonged to Satan had always persecuted those born of the promise and spirit (Christians):

*"Now we, brethren, as Isaac was, are the children of promise. But as then, he that was born after the flesh persecuted him that was born after the Spirit, even so it is now."*

*— Galatians 4:28-29*

Whereas the Apostle Paul had, by inspiration of God, declared that the Old Covenant given to Moses and the Israelites "decayeth" and is "vanishing away," Pope John Paul II repeatedly assured the Jews that the Word of God no longer mattered.

Rabbi David Rosen, a top official with the Vatican-founded, Conference of the Holy See Commission for Religious Relations with Jewry, wrote that he and a Jewish colleague met with Pope John Paul II in Assissi, Italy in January 1993. The Pope told Rosen: "I have said you (the Jewish people) are the beloved elder brothers of the original Covenant never broken and never to be broken."

Let's compare now: In the Holy Bible, Paul says that Jesus the Messiah came and gave mankind, including Jews, a *"new and better"* Covenant. As to the Old Covenant, Paul says it is decayed and vanishing. In disagreement with the Word of God, the usurper, Pope John Paul II says that the original Covenant is not broken and will never be broken! Who is the liar here?

### Visiting Our "Elder Brothers" in Christ

In 1986, John Paul II became the first Pope to ever visit and speak at the influential Synagogue in Rome. There he impressed the rabbis by referring to the Jews as *"the beloved elder brothers of the Church."*

Now "brothers" have a common father, and indeed, the Pope told the Jews they and Christians have the same Father. But, of course, the Apostles—Peter, Paul, and John to name just three—had warned the Jews that if they did not have the Son, Jesus, they did *not* have the Father, either. Jesus, in the Gospels, stated, *"I and the Father are One."*

Since the Jews hate and despise Jesus the Son, as their Talmud amply documents, who is their Father? Well, Jesus told the Jews: *"Ye are of your Father, the devil."* Obviously Pope John Paul II did not hesitate to curry favor with the Jews by making Jesus into a liar.

### Swallowed Up By Judaism and It's Accursed Gospel

All this is bad enough for it is proof that the Catholic Church has abandoned any semblance of true Christianity as taught by Jesus and the Apostles. In effect, what is called Christianity as found in the confines of the Roman Church, is swallowed up by Judaism. Rabbi Rosen is well aware of this. He writes (October 27, 2005) that the Pope's new teachings, first expressed in the papal encyclical *Nostra Aetate*, does not just reflect a transformation in attitude and teaching toward the Jews; it has profound implications for the Church in terms of its own theology." He continues:

> "Indeed, Pope Benedict XVI (successor to Pope John Paul II) himself has said that the Church has not yet fully discovered all the profound implications of *"Nostra Aetate."* Part of the reason for this lies in the very novelty of the Declaration. Cardinal Augustin Bea, at the time of the declaration's

promulgation, emphasized its groundbreaking nature."

Yes, just as the Rabbi says, the Vatican's new teachings are a "novelty," and they are "groundbreaking." They signal the absolute surrender of the Roman Catholic Church to the depths of Jewish satanism. In fact, what crypto-Jew Pope John Paul II, Pope Benedict XVI, and the current Pontiff, Pope Francis teach and insist the one billion Catholics embrace is exactly what *Galatians 3* in the New Testament flatly says is an "accursed" gospel.

> *"As we said before, so now I say again, If any man preach any other gospel unto ye than that ye have received, let him be accursed."*
> *— Galatians 1:9*

The Popes have labored incessantly to destroy the teaching that faith in Jesus Christ is essential for salvation. Their groundbreaking "novelty," "*Nostra Aetate*," returns things back to the way they were in Israel before Jesus Christ came in the flesh and before the New Covenant was given to humanity. Theirs is not the doctrine of Jesus' Gospel of the Kingdom but is instead the doctrine of the Jews' Kingdom.

The Popes tell the Christians they can earn their salvation by good works; they assure the Jews that the "works of the law" will suffice and that faith is not a pre-requisite. But again, what say the Scriptures? We read in *Galatians 3:9-13*...

> *"So then they which be of faith are blessed with faithful Abraham.*
>
> *"For as many as are of the works of the law are under the curse...*

*"But that no man is justified by the law in the sight of God, it is apparent: for, the just shall live by faith, And the law is not of faith…*

*"Christ hath redeemed us from the curse of the law…"*

The 21st century Popes are in rebellion against the very word and edicts of God! They encourage the Jews to pursue a path which guarantees they will remain *accursed* by God. They totally reject the entire New Testament and make no mention at all to the Jews of the finished work of Jesus on the cross. By teaching this satanic doctrine, the papacy mocks the resurrection of Christ, rejects the power of faith, and sends Jews straight to hell. As it says in *Galatians 3*, it is Christ who *redeems* people from the Curse, but the Popes teach that the Jews do not need Christ.

### *Catholic Doctrine to Change Further*

A wry observer might conclude that the Vatican has hidden motives in teaching this accursed doctrine. Could it be that the Popes in secret actually intend to deceive the Jews? Do they secretly detest and hate Jews so much they *desire* that they go to hell? That is the effect of their teachings—the end result. But a close examination of the facts does not bear this out. The "novelty" of "*Nostra Aetate*," the accursed doctrine first set in motion by Pope Paul VI and honed and sharpened by Pope John Paul II and now Popes Benedict XVI and Francis is a big step toward the *dissolution* of the Catholic Church altogether.

As Rabbi David Rosen emphasizes in quoting various papal authorities, the Vatican considers this novel teaching as but a skeleton upon which "more advanced" theology will be added. The skeleton will have more and more flesh and external parts attached until the whole creature is made visible. This will be a new Church of the Apocalypse. Rosen, naturally, loving the cave-in he is witnessing, congratulates the Vatican on its new teachings. He notes that the Pope believes "*Nostra Aetate*" to be "a world of Divine Wisdom" given the Pontiffs by God. But in truth, it is a doctrine of devils.

As has already happened in the Christian evangelical churches, Judaism and Jewry are being elevated to a state of superiority. Among Southern Baptists, members of the Assembly of God and Pentecostal churches, Jews are put on a pedestal. They are "God's Chosen," possessors of a superior external Covenant, destined to be rulers of Planet Earth; the Jews are "little gods," the "Apple of God's eye," favored in all respects by heaven. *Jewish Supremacism* is the latest innovation in Christendom and the "antiquated" teachings of Jesus and His Apostles is increasingly seen as unacceptable vestiges of anti-Semitism and bigotry.

### *Jesus Will Be Replaced*

Cries are already going up in Christian evangelical churches for a "Christian Talmud." Some ministers now teach from the Kabbalah. Jewish rabbis preach in Christian pulpits. The biblical concepts of Jesus as God are being reshaped and recast so that Jesus can be viewed by Christians everywhere as a good, reformist rabbi who never intended to leave the folds of Pharisaic Judaism. Jesus is being demoted, and in time—sooner than you can imagine—he will become an anachronism. Jesus will be seen as equivalent to say, a philosopher in Cicero, a Socrates, Milton, Voltaire, or an ancient days Billy Graham. But certainly he will not be God. In fact, Jesus' virulent anti-Semitism, the pastors and theologians will say, disqualifies him from being a role model for tolerant and loving 21st century "Christianity."

Who will replace Jesus as head of the Christian Church? The Pope no doubt already has replacement names ready—it could be of the Rabbinical sages Maimonides or Ben Eleazar; it could be the pioneer Israeli politicians David Ben Gurion, Shimon Perez, or Menachem Begin. Or the new prophets of Christianity could even be Vladimir Lenin or Karl Marx. Whoever is chosen to replace Jesus as "Lord" and "Redeemer," we know that all things will change.

We will certainly have more crypto-Jewish Popes who act as shills for Israel and Judaism. And there will be crypto-Jew evangelicals as well. Researchers have discovered Jewish blood ties, for example in evangelists Billy and Franklin Graham's ancestry which explains why Billy Graham has stated that Jews do not need to convert to Christianity. Flesh and blood Jews sitting on the papal throne and in the pulpits of America's mega churches will continue to revolutionize the church's doctrines until, indeed, all of Christendom is but a solid Jewish front. We are already not far from that grotesque day.

### *Prophecy to be Fulfilled*

The surprise, however, may be that a coming Pope will be Jewish but that his bloodline no longer kept secret. The Jewish "convert," Cardinal Jean Lustiger, from Paris, France was said to be a close competitor to the current German Cardinal Ratzinger, Pope Benedict XVI. Lustiger, being openly a professed Jew, was a close confidant of the late John Paul II. Sometime in the future, another Jew will present himself for election to the Holy See and the College of Cardinals will sweep him into office. He will end all pretenses that the Vatican and the Roman Catholic Church are followers of Jesus. He will exalt the House of Israel as holders and practitioners of the magical powers of Babylon. He will point the people of the world to the Jews as divine role models and claim that their Judaic holy books are law. And then the world will tilt and heads will role. Prophecy will be fulfilled.

Already the *Jewish Train* has left the station. The Pope is telling his one billion faithful—*"All Aboard!"* The John Hagees, the Richard Lands (of the Southern Baptist Convention), the Rick Warrens, and the Joel Osteens of the various evangelical affiliations have already jumped aboard and are seated in the passenger compartments. Zionism is the fuel and the Jews are the engineers in the locomotive speeding the train down the tracks.

### *"And I Will Carry You Away Beyond Babylon"*

This Zionist train filling up with passengers, emigrants from the once thriving but now depleted Christian Church—where is it taking its human cargo? We know that they have already left the parameters of Christianity. Their "Christian" leaders—the Popes, the Hagees, and Grahams—brought them as soul captives into the desolation of Judaism and earthly Zion. But their journey—and that of their Jewish overseers—has only begun. It started in Babylon long, long ago, spreading into Egypt, Greece, Rome, and far countries. But it will eventually end at a place called Armageddon.

The wonder of all this is that it was prophesied and by a very unlikely person inspired of God. I refer to Stephen, the first Christian martyr (other than Jesus Himself). In *Acts 6*, we find that Stephen had been set apart by the disciples of Jesus to be an evangelist and preacher of the Gospel: *"And Stephen, full of faith and power, did great wonders and miracles among the people."*

But his teaching and miracles greatly concerned the satanic leaders of the synagogue in Jerusalem. They conspired to set up false witnesses against him who accused Stephen of blasphemy against the holy place and the law. And so, the rabbis of the council summoned the young preacher before them and demanded he respond to these allegations. And Stephen, filled with the Holy Ghost, opened his mouth and the words of God were uttered to the council.

Stephen traced the history of the people of Israel from the call of God to Abraham till their betrayal and murder of Jesus. He recounted the many ways in which God had favored the people of Israel and yet they had repeatedly rebuffed the Lord and returned back to their ungodly Babylonian and Egyptian superstitions.

Stephen spoke, for example, of how God had miraculously brought them out of captivity in Egypt but, nevertheless, when Moses had departed to Mount Sinai where he received the tablets (the Ten Commandments,) during his absence the children of Israel were not faithful to God, but instead, in their wickedness had returned to the devilish, pagan religion of Egypt. Stephen's account of this tragic episode in the treacherous history of Israel was incredibly poignant and prophetic:

> *"This is that Moses...whom our Fathers would not obey, but thrust him out from them, and in their hearts turned back again into Egypt.*
>
> *"Saying unto Aaron, Make us gods to go before us: for as for this Moses, which brought us out of the land of Egypt, we wot not what is become of him.*
>
> *"And they made a calf in those days, and offered sacrifice unto the idol, and rejoiced in the works of their own hands.*
>
> *"Then God turned, and gave them up to worship the host of heaven; as it is written in the book of the prophets, O ye house of Israel, have ye offered to me slain beasts and sacrifices by the space of forty years in the wilderness?*
>
> *"Yea, ye took up the tabernacle of Moloch, and the star of your god Remphan, figures which ye made to worship them: and I will carry you away beyond Babylon."*
>
> *—Acts 7:37-43*

In these passages we learn that even as the Israelites

sacrificed to God, their hearts were in Egypt, lusting for the false gods, the sun god Osiris, the moon goddess Isis, their son Horus, and all the astrological hosts (deities and demonic entities) of heaven. And so they set up the golden calf representing Horus and other idols and began to worship them *even as they sacrificed slain beasts to the true God!* Their apostasy was made worse by this grotesque mixture.

## *This Apostasy Continues in the 21st Century*

Among the devils and idols worshipped as gods by the Israelites were Moloch, the hideous god to whom sacrifices of children in the fires were made, and the god Remphan, whose image was the star—the very star that, today, Jews adore and which is the symbol found prominently displayed on the national flag of Israel.

This is the spiritually corrupt pattern repeated over and over by physical Israel and the Jews over the centuries. They pretend to worship the true God in heaven but in truth lustfully follow after the ancient gods of the Mystery religion of Babylon and Egypt. In this, the 21st century, the Jews continue to perpetuate this hybrid, Satanic religious porridge. The rabbis lay claim to their belief in the Torah, the first five books of the Old Testament. But in fact, they make void the Torah and the Word of God by their man-made traditions, as outlined in the Talmud and in other "holy books."

To make matters worse, the Jewish zealots have not ceased to adore and worship the star of their god, Remphan, whose image is superimposed on their flag, and they enthusiastically worship the "host of heaven." How so? Because of their teaching and practice of the Kabbalah which contains doctrines of hell, including the use of sorcery, astrology, and magic and introduces a multiplicity of sex gods and goddesses. The ultimate, of course, is that the learned rabbis of Kabbalah present to the modern-day House of Israel a god whom they believe is destined to lead them out of the wilderness and into the pinnacle of world power. That god, whom the Jews shower with precious stones, pearls, gold, silver and other wealth, is named *Leviathan*. He is, incredulously the Serpent.

In their most secret of doctrines, the teaching preserved throughout the ages and now garnished and polished as the gem of Judaic belief, the Serpent, Leviathan, shall, they believe, catapult the Jews into their long, lusted for Kingdom, reigning over planet earth and making all Gentiles bow at their feet.

Did not God through his prophet and martyr, Stephen, not prophesy and declare:

*"AND I WILL CARRY YOU AWAY BEYOND BABYLON."*

Beyond Babylon! The Judaic religion proceeded out of Babylon and to this day is pure Babylonian in traditions and doctrine, and ritual. But God will empower the Devil further. He will take the Jews—and their Judaizer associates and accomplices in the Catholic Church and in pro-Zionist evangelical Christendom—even farther. Their destiny shall be found "Beyond Babylon."

TWELVE
_____

**Prophetic Destiny: Ten Afflictions Assigned The House of Israel (World Jewry) Because of It's Apostasy and Rebellion**

# The House of Israel—Accursed and Bewitched

"For the Lord of hosts hath purposed, and who shall disannul it? and his hand is stretched out, and who shall turn it back?"
—*Isaiah 15:27*

"As we said before, so say I now again, if any man preach any other gospel unto you that ye have received, let him be accursed."
—*Galatians 1:9*

**W**orld Jewry, in rebellion and apostate, is engaged in a long-running and fateful conspiracy. This ages-old conspiracy inspired and led by Satan and his devils is destined to end tragically for the Jewish people, as well as for those Gentiles who throw their lot in with the Jews in pursuing its satanic goals.

By "World Jewry" I mean all—men and women—who say they are Jews, claiming such by either genetics (race) or by virtue of religion. As we shall see, World Jewry has other distinguishing characteristics as well.

Many who claim to be Jews and say they are Jews are not actually "Jews" in scientific fact. Their DNA is not of ancient Israelite origins. The Khazars, a nation and people of Mongol/Turkish stock who converted to Judaism during the 8th and 9th Centuries, later migrated mainly to Russia and Europe but also to other nations around the globe in smaller numbers. Called "Ashkenazis," many of the Khazars immigrated to modern Israel (Palestine) after World War II are "Jews," but only by virtue of their professed claims.

### *The Synagogue of Satan is Not the "Israel of God"*

*Revelation 2* and *3* speak of the *Synagogue of Satan*, made up of "them which say they are Jews and are not." This term "Synagogue of Satan" certainly refers to the Khazars who today make up the majority of "Jews" living in the physical nation of Israel. But the term Synagogue of Satan also incorporates all who truly are of the lineage of the 12 tribes of Israel. They also are "them which say they are Jews and are not." This is because in the scriptures it is made clear that a true Jew is one who spiritually has faith in Jesus Christ, the Messiah of Israel. Such a person is "born again" and spiritually is made a citizen of heavenly Jerusalem; joining other Christians who, collectively, are the Holy Israel of God.

The *Israel of God*, then, is a spiritual nation, made up of born again men and women—physically either Jew *or* Gentile—who are, in fact, collectively "Abraham's seed" and are heirs according to the promise given Abraham *(Galatians 3:16 and 26-19)*. That promise is Jesus, who alone is the Saviour, Messiah, and Blessed Hope of Israel. Jews who have this promise in their hearts are not part of the Synagogue of Satan but have been rescued from God's judgement of the Jews. They are in opposition to the Zionist goal of global domination, reject Jewish Supremacism, and the apostasy of Judaism.

### *The Destiny of World Jewry—Ten Afflictions to Befall Jews Who Have Rejected Jesus*

*World Jewry* is comprised of Jews who have rejected Jesus and who loathe the reality of His being their Saviour (Messiah). Their Talmud, their most sacred book, alleges Jesus to be an imposter, a blasphemer, and a "destroyer of Israel."

They are the spiritual—and perhaps in some cases, physical—descendants of those who, in the days of Pilate and Jesus, cried out, *"Crucify Him! Crucify Him!"* Today, World Jewry insists, "We will not have this man (Jesus) rule over us." In fact, World Jewry is a counterfeit "Israel," which once crucified and to this day rejects its Saviour and Messiah, Jesus Christ.

And so, the stage is set for disaster. World Jewry (earthly and physical "Israel"), being apostate and in rebellion to God, must fulfill its prophetic destiny. That destiny is tragic, indeed, for God has assigned *"Ten Afflictions"* to befall the Jews. It is imperative that we examine these Ten Afflictions because our own destiny and future stand out in sharp contrast to that of the Jews.

They, the Jews of World Jewry and counterfeit "Israel," are unquestionably history's troublemakers; they have been the tormentors of humanity and persecutors of Christianity for two millennia. The Curse of Cain is spiritually attached to the Jews. As we shall see, World Jewry tragically is both *accursed* and *bewitched*. The scriptures conclusively demonstrate that this is so. Let us, then, begin our investigation into the *Ten Afflictions Assigned Israel* (World Jewry) *Because of Its Apostasy and Rebellion*. Please remember as we discuss these Ten afflictions that though we speak of the "Jews," we exclude those Jews who are *not* of World Jewry, who are instead spiritually separated from its conduct and its destiny and who know Jesus Christ as Lord and Saviour.

### *Affliction Number One: Turned Over to the Devil*

There are over 300 prophecies in the Old Testament that point to the coming of Jesus Christ the Messiah. But when the Messiah came 2000 years ago, the Jews, engrossed in their oral Talmudic traditions, were oblivious to His coming. Wrapped in selfishness, lust for money and their hatred of humanity, neither could they envision a Messiah who focused not on material things, but on the spiritual heights of love and kindness. The Jews looked for a new King David, a warrior-king who would pridefully lead the superior-race Jews in conquering the world and making the Jews rich and powerful. Instead, Jesus came as a humble servant, teaching the beatitudes, asking his disciples to deny themselves and follow Him.

Moreover, this man Jesus preached a New Covenant which replaced the old and which was diametrically opposite the Pharisees Talmudic religion. No, this was not the "King" for whom the vast majority of worldly Jews sought to guide them into a Jewish Utopia. Jesus was rejected of the chief rabbis, turned over to Pilate for execution, and crucified on the cross.

This heinous crime and also the Jews' *apostasy* of deserting the Old Covenant of Moses and embracing the man-made Traditions of the Elders (Satan's Talmud), stamped physical Israel and the Jews as in *rebellion* to God and His laws. For this apostasy and rebellion, Jesus ordained Ten Afflictions. The first, precedent to all others, is Jesus' declaration that Israel and the Jews had been *turned over to the Devil for destruction*. He accused them, saying they were *"hypocrites," "fools," "blind guides," "full of extortion and excess," "whited sepulchers full of dead mean's bones and all uncleaness..." (Matthew 23)*.

Then, Jesus said bluntly to the Jews *(Matthew 23:31-32)*:

*"Wherefore ye be witnesses unto yourselves, That ye*

*are the children of them which killed the prophets.*

*"Fill ye up then the measure of your fathers*

*"Ye serpents, ye generation* (race or ethnic group) *of vipers, how can ye escape the damnation of Hell?"*

Again as recorded in *John 8:44*, Jesus said to the Jews: *"Ye are of your father the Devil..."*

This, then is Affliction Number One—Israel and the Jews are turned over to their father, the devil, for damnation.

### Affliction Number Two: Possessed by Spirits of Money, Sorcery, Murder, Hatred, Sexual Perversions and Filth

Having been turned over to the Devil, a punishment confirmed and meted out by Jesus, the Jews sank into a condition of reprobate mind. Their father, the Devil, possessed the Jews and they have even been overcome by inordinate lust for money, driven by hatred to murder, and consumed with a disgusting mindset and lifestyle of filth and degradation. These evils are plagues visited upon the Jewish people related to their adoption of their satanic Talmudic religion. Satanic possession of the Jews accelerated with their rejection of Jesus the Messiah and their cruel mockery of His redemptive sacrifice on the cross.

### The Spirit of Money

In regard to *money*, Jesus pleaded with the Jews:

*"Lay not up for yourselves treasures upon earth, where moth and rust doth corrupt, and where thieves break through and steal:*

*"But lay up for yourselves treasures in heaven...*

*"For where your treasure is, there will your heart be also."*

*—Matthew 6:19-21*

Jesus gave the Jews the *Parable of Lazarus and the Rich Man*. A story in which the faithful but poverty-stricken beggar was rewarded with heaven but the greedy rich man ended up in a burning hell. In another parable He commended the widow who unselfishly had given her tiny offering, a mite, while he berated the rich man who beat his breasts and boasted of all he had given. Jesus advised the rich, young ruler, "give to the poor all your riches and come, follow me." Christ warned His disciples that it is easier for a camel to go through the eye of a needle than for a rich man to enter the kingdom of heaven.

He Himself had not even a fox hole to lay His head—no mansion, no servant, even though Jesus was God incarnate and could have commanded anything he desired. He chose to suffer all temptations and to live the humble life of the poor.

The Jews would agree to none of it. Indeed, Jesus, they reasoned, could not be the Messiah, else He would be wealthy and powerful. No King comes as a servant.

### *"Ye Cannot Serve God and Mammon"*

Jesus, discerning their hearts, knew of their lust for money and so He set forth a stunning choice for them. On one side was God; on the other, Mammon or money. Now "mammon" means the wealth and material goods of the world. Literally, this word mammon refers to the riches given by virtue of man's worship of the Great Goddess of the ancient world, of Babylon, Egypt, Rome and Greece. "Mam" stood for this divine feminine deity, "mon" for the world. Therefore, Jesus said:

> *"No man can serve two masters: For either he will hate the one and love the other: or else he will hold to the one, and despise the other. Ye cannot serve God and mammon."*

"Ye cannot serve God and mammon," those were Jesus' words. And history shows that of the two, the Jews chose their preferred master, the Babylonian solution: *mammon.*

This was earlier prophesied by the prophet Daniel while captive in Babylon. In a vision, Daniel saw the last days wicked "King" of Israel and the whole world. This would be the same personage described in *Revelation 13* as the man with the number 666, the endtimes world leader, or antichrist. Daniel's prophetic vision is recorded in *Daniel 11:36-39*:

> *"And the king shall do according to his will; and he shall exalt himself, and magnify himself above every god, and shall speak marvellous things against the God of gods, and shall prosper till the indignation be accomplished: for that that is determined shall be done.*
>
> *"Neither shall he regard the God of his fathers, nor the desire of women, nor regard any god: for he shall magnify himself above all.*
>
> *"But in his estate shall he honour the God of forces: and a god whom his fathers knew not shall he honour with gold, and silver, and with precious stones, and pleasant things.*
>
> *"Thus shall he do in the most strong holds with a strange god, whom he shall acknowledge and increase with glory: and he shall cause them to rule over many, and shall divide the land for gain."*

Yes, Israel and the Jews chose mammon over God, a strange god whom their fathers, Moses and the Prophets, knew not. The Jews, choosing money as their god, went on to crucify the very Son of God. The spirit of money had possessed the Jews and they were in its fast grip. Is this not why many Jews have over the centuries given themselves names such as Coppersmith, Silver, Silverstein, Gold, Goldman, Goldberg, Goldstein,

Diamond, and Rubenstein (Ruby Stone)?

Is this not also the reason why Rothschild and other Jews have for ages been enamored with banking, finance, and money? Are such men not "gifted" by their ruling spirits with a King Midas love of and compulsion for making money? Is Wall Street, the Mecca of money, not the exclusive preserve of rich Jews?

## *Talmud Focuses on Money*

Is this also why, in their Talmud, money and the making of money is a prime, repeated topic and why the Talmud instructs the Jews that they should feel free to cheat and deceive Gentiles in commerce and rob them of their money? Is it why the Talmud assures the Jews that all the wealth of the Gentiles shall someday be theirs?

Paul, writing to the younger disciple, Timothy, warned that, *"The love of money is the root of all evil." (Timothy 6:10)* It is

The Jews' obsession with money is even seen on the U.S. one dollar bill, which has a Jewish six-pointed star displayed over the Great Seal of the eagle.

not, therefore, that money is intrinsically evil, but that an inordinate lust for and love of money *is* the *root* of *all* evil.

Unrepentent Jews are evil, and at the root of their diseased imaginations is their love of money.

### *Spirits That Inspire Crave Lusts and Demonism*

There are, however, other craven lusts which engage the energy and attention of Jews. Demonic spirits which inspire sorcery, murder, hatred, sexual perversions, and filth are prevalent. It is not that the Gentiles do not have these same lusts, many do. But the Jews are especially afflicted with such unbecoming satanic lusts and desires.

Sorcery, history has demonstrated, is a vile and curious art in which the Jews have excelled. Their Kabbalah, integrated into Judaic religion by the rabbis, is replete with magic and sorcery. Research any of a number of occult dictionaries and encyclopedias and you will discover that Jewish witches, sorcerers, and shamans have been the foremost leaders in the field of sorcery. Astrology, necromancy, numerology, divination, tarot cards—in all these and more the Jews have been the utmost purveyors of evil.

Albert Pike, former Sovereign Grand Commander of the Scottish Rite and author of Freemasonry's classic textbook, *Morals and Dogma*, admits therein that all the rituals and doctrines of the Masonic Lodge are based on the Jewish Kabbalah. In June, 1966, a Jew, Anton Szandor LaVey, founded the Church of Satan in California; today, the biography of the world's best known witch, Miriam Starhawk, admits she is a Jewess.

### *Satan in the Talmud*

We have already seen Jesus' curse on the Jews as the ones responsible for the murder of all the righteous blood ever shed on planet earth. In their most holy book, the Talmud, we discover an inordinate, persistent, sick focus on hatred of people

> **PUBLIC AUCTION.**
> By Permission of Charles Lining, esq. Ordinary for Charleston District, will be sold on TUESDAY, 25th inst. before the Subscribers auction store, without reserve,
> The following NEGROES,
> Belonging to the estate of Madam Galucha, deceased:
> A NEGRO WENCH, about 30 years of age, a good cook, washer and ironer, and a faithful servant.
> ALSO,
> A NEGRO MAN, about 48 years of age, a good dray-man and is somewhat of a cook; both warranted sober, honest and no run-aways. Conditions, cash.
> By order of the Executors,
> Jacob Cohen & Co.
> October 19.

As this old newspaper ad demonstrates that Jewish slave traders were responsible for the slave industry in the United States. Judah P. Benjamin, Confederate Secretary of State, was a Jew who owned more than 50 slaves on his southern plantation.

of other races. We also find a sanctioning of the murder of Gentiles and of all supposed "enemies" of the Jews.

We see, too, in the Talmud an excess of attention directed to sexual perversions, ranging from the approval of adultery, sodomy, pederasty or pedophilia (sex with children), necrophilia (sex with the dead), coprophilia (sex acts using human excretion and waste), and bestiality (sex with animals).

There is also excessive attention in Talmudic tractates (sections) paid to toilet behavior and bodily functions—menstruation, penis erection, vaginal cleanliness, etc.

Christians would be aghast if they but knew of the despicable nature of the Jews' Talmud. Regrettably, they are kept in the dark by the rabbis and by their own deceived leadership.

In my eye-opening documentary video, *Cauldron of Abaddon—From Jerusalem and Israel Flow a Torrent of Satanic Evil and Mischief Endangering the Whole World*, I examine the undeniably corrupt lifestyles of the Jews providing ample evidence that Jews are behind the great majority of the world's illegal drugs, pornography, mafia/mob activity, prostitution, sex slavery, and other ills. No other race, no other nation is in such dire bondage to demon spirits, and no other race and nation, has similarly plagued the entire world with such a disgusting array of body and soul-destroying toxins.

When God turned the Jews over to Satan, they were possessed body and soul by hellish spirits and that possession has resulted in a damaged world population scarred and made desperate with sin, misery, and degradation.

### *Affliction Number Three: Guilty of all the Blood Ever Shed on Planet Earth*

Jesus declared in *John 8:44, "Ye are of your father the devil," and he went on to say: "and the lusts of your father ye will do. He was a murderer from the beginning..."*

Now here is the summation: The Jews are declared the sons and daughters of the Devil (i.e. Satan). He was a murderer from the beginning. Therefore, by extension, the Jews are partakers spiritually of these murders. Like father, like son, in a manner of speaking. Can this be so? Can the Jews be adjudged guilty and responsible for all the murders, all blood shed on earth, since the first, when wicked Cain slew his righteous brother, Abel? Read, now, Jesus' judgement:

> *"Fill ye up the measure of your fathers... wherefore, behold, I send unto you prophets, and wise men, and scribes: and some of them ye shall kill and crucify; and some of them shall ye scourge in your synagogues, and persecute them from city to city.*
>
> *"That upon you may come all the righteous blood shed upon the earth, from the blood of righteous Abel...*
>
> *"Verily I say unto you, all these things shall come upon this generation* (the House of Israel).
>
> *"O Jerusalem Jerusalem, thou that killest the prophets."*

Yes, Jesus' righteous judgement is that the House of Israel (see *Matthew 23:37-38*) is guilty of "all the righteous blood shed upon the earth, from the blood of righteous Abel."

### The Fall of that Great City, Mystery Babylon the Great

Now, the scriptures are designed so that such powerful and momentous declarations and judgements as this are almost always repeated and/or reinforced. Thus, in *Revelation 18*, we are told of the falling of that "Great City" spiritually called "Babylon the Great": *"For her sins have reached unto heaven, and God hath remembered her for her iniquities"* (*vs. 5*). This great city is none other than Jerusalem, which is the Great City of the House of Israel. That this is so is proven many times in scripture.

The Old Testament prophets called Israel "Babylon" and pronounced her a "whore." Peter, head of the Christian Church at Jerusalem, wrote a letter to Christians and the salutation read:

A billboard announcing the 1962 movie, *Sodom and Gomorrah*. Today, the gays and transgenders would protest such a movie, yet the Bible prophesies that Jerusalem and Israel shall be as Sodom and Egypt in the last days. Tel Aviv was rated as the world's number one "gay friendly city" by the travel industry and a gigantic gay festival and parade is held there every year in celebration.

*"The church that is at Babylon elected together with you, saluteth you..." (I Peter 5:13)*. This could only have been referring to Jerusalem, where Peter lived and preached. At that time, the ancient physical city of Babylon, in Sumaria (modern-day Iraq) lay in ruins.

Another proof is that in *Revelation 11:9*, Jerusalem is called that "Great City." This city is further described as *"the Great City, which spiritually is called Sodom and Egypt, where also our Lord was crucified."*

What a statement of evil! Jerusalem is a Great City in terms of its wickedness, being spiritually comparable to *"Sodom and Egypt!"* More on this later.

In *Revelation 18*, we find this Great City, Jerusalem (spiritual Sodom and Egypt) as having a global dominion: *"For all the nations have drunk of the wrath of her fornication, and the kings of the earth committed fornication with her, and the merchants of the earth are waxed rich through the abundance of her delicacies..."*

### A Worldwide Trading System

This Great City, also spiritually code-named "Mystery, Babylon the Great," is further depicted in *Revelation 18* as being the organizer of a worldwide economic trading system. Every product imaginable, from perfumes to precious metals, agricultural products and animals, are traded and the merchants of the earth have prospered and grown rich, as ships full of cargo traverse the seas importing and exporting these goods.

What we have here is a picture of our twenty-first century world, a world of commerce and finance in which the Jewish bankers, the Wall Street cartel, and its many offshoots—from London to Shanghai and Rio de Janeiro—have made World Jewry (the House of Israel) dominant and ubiquitous. The rise of World Jewry to global economic mastery over the past 2000 years—just as was prophesied—has truly been spectacular.

But, God has ordained the resounding *fall* of this Great City;

with massive violence it shall be thrown down, and Heaven will rejoice at its sudden, total destruction.

### Merchants of Deceit, Sorcery, and Blood

Why this severe judgement on the Jews' House of Israel, symbolized as that Great City which we know to be Jerusalem? *Revelation 18:23-24* provides the sure explanation for God's harsh judgement on this wicked, planetary-trading metropolis ruled by Jewish money men:

> *"for thy merchants were the great men of the earth: for by thy sorceries were all nations deceived.*
>
> *"And in her was found the blood of prophets, and of saints, and of all that were slain upon the earth."*

Thus did Jesus Christ, the "Spirit of Prophecy" *(Revelation 19:10)*, accuse that "Great City, Mystery Babylon the Great," of being responsible for the "blood of prophets, and of saints and of all that were slain upon the earth." Now compare this indictment in *Revelation 18:23-24* with that of Jesus in *Matthew 23:34-36* when he righteously accuses the House of Israel and the Jews of the monstrous crime:

> *"Wherefore, behold, I send unto you prophets and wise men, and scribes: and some of them ye shall kill and crucify...*
>
> *"That upon you may come all the righteous blood shed upon the earth, from the blood of righteous Abel..."*

*Matthew 23* and *Revelation 18* are virtually identical, both being in the form of divine accusations against "the House of Israel" (i.e. the Jews), being adjudged *"Guilty of all the righteous blood ever shed on planet earth."* Punishment surely is due for these crimes committed by those who, like their father, the Devil, are mass murderers. That punishment leads us to the next great affliction assigned to the unrepentant Jews.

## Affliction Number Four: The Old Covenant is Broken and Replaced

Their being found guilty of past and future murders and continuing in their apostasy and rebellion, God has severed the Old Covenant He made with the House of Israel. Again and again, God laid down the conditions by which Israel could retain and remain in this Holy Covenant. But repeatedly, the people of Israel rebelliously refused to abide by these conditions and instead "went a whoring after false gods," including the god of self-idolatry, as revealed in abundance in the Jews' Babylonian Talmud, the traditions of the elders which Jesus so roundly condemned. Therefore, God *divorced* Israel, ended the Covenant forever; and meted out punishment for their transgressions.

Isaiah said of the backslidden and rebellious people of Israel, *"He hath broken the covenant...and the people shall be as the burnings of lime: as thorns cut up shall they be burned in the fire."* Isaiah *(33:8-14)* further prophesied:

> *"The sinners in Zion are afraid; fearfulness hath surprised the hypocrites. Who among us shall dwell with the devouring fire? Who among us shall dwell with everlasting burnings?"*

## They Conspired Against God

This prophecy is further elaborated in *Isaiah 11:1-14*, where the Prophet declares that Israel (including Judah and Jerusalem) has not kept the Covenant but has been disobedient to God:

> *"Yet they obeyed not nor inclined their ear, but walked everyone in the imagination of their evil heart: therefore I will bring upon them all the words of this*

*covenant, which I commanded them to do, but they did them not.*

*"And the Lord said unto me, a conspiracy is found among the men of Judah, and among the inhabitants of Jerusalem.*

*"They are turned back to the iniquities of their forefathers, which (also) refused to hear my words; and they went after other gods, to serve them: the house of Israel and the house of Judah have broken my covenant...*

*"Therefore thus saith the Lord, Behold, I will bring evil upon them, which they shall not be able to escape...*

*"Therefore pray not for this people, neither lift up a prayer for them: for I will not hear them in the time that they cry unto me for their trouble."*

### The New Covenant Offered to Gentiles and Jews

We know, then, that the Jews became so evil—and are so today—that they *conspired* against God and His anointed and were afflicted with evil hearts. Still, a *remnant* will be saved, made up of those who are chosen by Jesus Christ and have faith in Him. This tiny remnant, having repented of their transgressions, will be grafted back in to the Tree of Life, even though the House of Israel, the vast majority of Jews, have been cut off by God and are lost forever. The Jews who make up the saved remnant join the Gentiles who believe in Jesus. Together, these believers (the "Israel of God") are brought into the New Covenant. The Old Covenant was torn asunder in the days of the Apostles, and so Jesus made a New Covenant with His Chosen, the Gentiles and Jews who are His own and are now exclusively "Abraham's seed:"

*"And if ye be Christ's, then are ye Abraham's seed, and heirs according to the promise."*
*— Galatians 3:29*

Of this New (and better) Covenant, Paul, in *Galatians 8:6-13*, wrote:

*"But now hath he* (Jesus) *obtained* (for us, Christians, the true Israel of God) *a more excellent ministry by how much also he is the mediator of a better covenant, which was established on better promises."*

*"For if that first covenant had been faultless, then should no place have been sought for the second...*

*"In that he* (Jesus) *saith, a new covenant, he hath made the first old. Now that which decayeth and waxeth old is ready to vanish away."*

With the sacrifice of Jesus on the cross and his shedding of blood, the redemption of His chosen people—Christians saved through faith—became a reality. The Gospel began to be preached to the whole world, and the New Covenant was firmly in place.

Affliction Number Four was assigned to the apostate and rebellious "House of Israel:" *The Old Covenant is broken and replaced.*

### Affliction Number Five: The House of Israel is Left Desolate

Immediately after placing a righteous curse on the House of Israel, that curse being their guilt of murdering throughout history all the righteous, Jesus decreed a punishment to be levied on the Jews:

*"O Jerusalem, Jerusalem, thou that killest the prophets, and stonest them which are sent unto thee,*

*how often would I have gathered thy children together, even as a hen gathereth her chickens under her wings, and ye would not!*

*"Behold, your house is left unto you desolate.*

*"For I say unto you, Ye shall not see me henceforth, till ye shall say, Blessed is he that cometh in the name of the Lord."*
— *Matthew 23:37-39*

Note Jesus' declarative prophecy: *"Behold, your house is left unto you desolate."* What does the word "desolate" mean? This describes a void; nothing left of value, Israel is spiritually deserted and abandoned. Indeed, the moment Jesus died on the cross, the veil of the temple in Jerusalem was ripped in two from top to bottom. The Spirit of God had departed and the glory of His presence was not found in the land *(Matthew 27:51-53).*

Israel was left desolate, and Jesus prophesied this desolation would continue until He returns. Therefore, the return of the Jews to Palestine and the founding of counterfeit Israel in 1948 was in direct disobedience to Jesus. He stated that Israel would be *"left desolate"* until His return. The Jews who defied Jesus and set up this grotesque caricature of a Holy City were in rebellion in doing so. The Christians who assisted them in this ungodly endeavor to *undo* what Jesus had done should be ashamed.

Arrogance and pride is evident among the supposed Christians who praise and embrace this satanic nation of apostate and rebellious Jews. In no way is this a "Holy City" or a "Holy Land." It is, instead, a spear point of rebellion against God, a city in which the prophesied *"Abomination of Desolation"* will occur and Israel's pitiful fate will be sealed:

*"But when ye shall see the Abomination of Desolation,*

BLOOD COVENANT WITH DESTINY   〇   179

This is the note that President Obama left at the crack in the wailing wall when he visited Jerusalem. This witchcraft voodoo practice is an insult and affront to God who states in *Matthew* in the Bible, that He has taken the Kingdom from the Jews and that the house of Israel is left desolate.

*spoken of by Daniel the prophet, standing where it ought not, (let him that readeth understand) then let them that be in Judah flee to the mountains... For in those days shall be affliction, such as was not from the beginning of the creation..."*
—*Mark 13: 14-19*

In sum: Twenty-first century Israel is a squalid place of *spiritual desolation* exactly as Jesus said it would be. To re-paraphrase that old saying made the more famous recently by Sarah Palin in her Vice-Presidential nominee acceptance speech at the Republican Party National Convention in 2007, "You can put lipstick on a pig but it is still a pig."

Israel is "left desolate," and its increasing tally of modern-day sins and crimes mark it as such. The House of Israel is a despicable failure; it is the greedy pig among the world's nations that eventually shall find itself on the menu of those who eat pork.

### *Affliction Number Six: Destruction of the Temple*

The Temple of God being defiled by the Jews and their religion, Jesus decreed and prophesied that Herod's Temple in Jerusalem would be thrown down and not a stone would be left standing. In 70 A.D., the Roman General Titus, on orders from Caesar, totally destroyed the city of Jerusalem and supervised the utter destruction of their Temple. Jesus' prophecy came true.

Since that day, the Jews have repeatedly sought and schemed to rebuild their Temple in Jerusalem, but have had no success. Today, the Jews continue their futile quest, despite the fact that Moslems built their great golden-domed Mosque of Omar on or very near the site where the Jews' Temple once stood. It may well be that World War III will be initiated with the bogus modern-day nation of Israel blowing up and destroying the Moslem Holy Place and mosque so that the Jewish Temple can be built on its ashes and debris.

Tragically, a number of deceived evangelical Christians are complicit in the Jewish plot to rebuild the Temple. They think they are doing God service, blessing the Jews and hastening the day when Jesus will return. In reality, what they are doing is rebelling against God and defying His Word. They foolishly seek to help the Jews *undo* what God hath done.

### *The Antichrist to Come*

Jesus prophesied that the Temple would be destroyed and that the House of Israel would be *"left desolate"* until the day He returns. But these arrogant and rebellious "Judeo-Christians" defiantly seek to rebuild that same destroyed Temple, and they work diligently to prosper and grow physical Israel in absolute defiance of Jesus' Word. What shall be the consequence of their unholy defiance?

The Apostle Paul, in *II Thessalonians 2*, provides the

shocking prophetic answer. In a future rebuilt Temple in Jerusalem, a counterfeit Messiah of the Jews shall someday show himself. Paul warns Christians that this evil man may appear to be a Messiah and that some might imagine that Christ himself has returned. But, don't be deceived, Paul writes, he shall, instead, be *"that man of sin...the son of perdition:"*

> *"Let no man deceive you by any means: for that day shall not come, except there come a falling away first, and that man of sin be revealed, the son of perdition;*
>
> *"Who opposeth and exalteth himself above all that is called God, or that is worshipped; so that he as God sitteth in the temple of God, shewing himself that he is God...*
>
> *"For the mystery of iniquity doth already work: only he who now letteth will let, until he be taken out of the way.*
>
> *"And then shall that Wicked be revealed, whom the Lord shall consume with the spirit of his mouth, and shall destroy with the brightness of his coming:*
>
> *"Even him, whose coming is after the working of Satan with all power and signs and lying wonders,*
>
> *"And with all deceivableness of unrighteousness in them that perish; because they received not the love of the truth, that they might be saved.*
>
> *"And for this cause God shall send them strong delusion, that they should believe a lie:*
>
> *"That they all might be damned who believed not the truth, but had pleasure in unrighteousness."*
>            *—II Thessalonians 3-12*

What a turnabout! The Jews expect their Messiah, the new King David, to come and reign over a "Jewish Utopia" kingdom. The Jews believe that they shall all live like royalty, lording it over the Gentiles, piling up into their coffers the wealth of the entire globe. But instead of a new King David, a man possessed by Satan, known as the "son of perdition," shall appear, declaring he alone is God and requiring the Jews and the whole world to worship him!

Thus, the deceived and foolish "Christians" who endeavor to help the Jews conquer one of their most formidable earthly enemies, the Moslems, and who are assisting the Jews in their degenerate plan to rebuild their destroyed Temple, are actually helping Satan and His antichrist come to power and set up an earthly throne.

Oh what a grotesque invention can take shape and end in terror when God is not its author.

### *Affliction Number Seven: Dispersion into the Wilderness*

Six afflictions have been laid on the heads of the Jews, now comes a seventh—their banishment from Jerusalem and Israel and being dispersed throughout the world. The Jews call this the "Diaspora."

I need not belabor the point that the Old Testament prophets as well as Jesus prophesied this tragic event. In his classic text, *Rise and Fall of the Roman Empire*, British historian Edward Gibbon detailed how the dispersion of the Jews took place after a lengthy series of conflicts between the Jews and the Greeks and Romans. Everywhere in the Roman Empire, Jews rose up and began to kill their neighbors. In Cyprus and Cyrene, Jews cruelly tortured and massacred hundreds of thousands of innocent men, women, and children. Never had the citizens of the Roman Empire experienced such savagery, such inhumanity. The Jews took pleasure in killing Gentiles. They ate human flesh and danced wildly around their victims' carcasses. They were like vicious banshees and devils from another dimension celebrating their victories.

The Roman Caesar was sickened to hear eyewitness accounts of the Jews' merciless conduct. He ordered his generals to make war on Israel and all Jews, to burn their capital, Jerusalem, and to tear down every stone of their ungodly Temple, wherein the rabbis plotted to carry out their fierce rebellion.

## *The Destruction of Jerusalem*

In 70 AD, General Titus completed the decimation of Jerusalem, slew hundreds of thousands, took many survivors hostage as slaves, and shut down the city, making it off limits and forbidden to be rebuilt.

Many hundreds of thousands of Jews fled Israel and were saved. But wherever they went in the Empire, when identified as "those horrible Jews," they were forced into involuntary servitude.

They became the pariahs of the civilized world, not because they were Jews but because they were widely recognized as troublemakers, hucksters, devil worshippers, murderers, and thieves.

At that time, the word "anti-Semitism" had not been invented. Nevertheless, we can say with certitude that whatever hatred and animosity the people felt against the Jews, it was well earned. That is not blind racism or anti-Semitism; rather, it is a matter of self-protection and cautious watchfulness in light of the inhuman barbarism practiced by the Jews.

Such is also invariably the case today, in the 21st century, with the barbaric behavior of Jews everywhere igniting emotions of despair, panic, and dislike on the part of Gentiles who know of their dastardly evils and fiendish conduct. Just to understand the sinister depths of their fanatical religion and its Talmud holy book instills fear and loathing by compassionate and gentle men and women everywhere.

## Modern Israel is Born with U.S. and Soviet Help

As for the destroyed city, Jerusalem and its once magnificent edifice, Herod's Temple, over the centuries the dispersed Jews have on several occasions sought to return and restore their lost habitat. But their efforts never enjoyed even partial success until the twentieth century. In 1948, the nation of Israel became a reality. By that time, three factors empowered the foreign, dispersed Jews to invade Palestine, seize lands of the native-born Palestinians, and found the newest version of Israel:

1. The Jews used their clannish rabbinical communities in Europe as launching pads to seize, steal, or earn considerable riches from generally unsuspecting Gentiles;

2. The Jews employed the advantages that came their way from control of America's White House (particularly the Wilson, FDR, and Truman administrations) and its banks, Federal Reserve System, and Wall Street firms; and

3. The Soviet Union, founded by savage Communist Jews (Lenin, Trotsky, and others), in 1917 favored the Ashkenazi Jews' and later, after World War II, assisted the Jewish terrorists who were seeking to conquer Palestine with arms and by diplomatic means.

## Hitler a Godsend to the Jews?

There is now abundant evidence that from 1932-1944, Zionist leaders in the United States, Britain, and Europe covertly aided Hitler and Germany as the Nazis worked to depopulate Europe of Jews and transfer them to a new homeland. The Zionists, especially the wealthy Samuel Untermyer and the influential Rabbi Stephen Wise in the United States, believed that most Jews, unassimilated yet residing safely ensconced and living comfortably and often in luxury in Germany and Europe, would

> **The Transfer Agreement**, by Edwin Black, is one of many books documenting that the Zionist Jews had secret arrangements with the Nazis for Jews to be allowed to immigrate to Palestine in 1933 and take much of their their money and assets with them.

never voluntarily resettle to a backward Middle Eastern territory like Palestine. Hitler, in their eyes, was a godsend. Jewish representatives worked closely and clandestinely with Himmler, Heydrich, and other Nazis to effect an orderly transfer.

Today, demographers report that there are fewer than 19 million Jews in all the world. About 7.5 million of them reside in Israel and an equal number in the United States. Britain and Continental Europe have many of the remainder, though scattered pockets of Jews are found in Australia, New Zealand, in Mexico, Central and South America, in Canada, in the Orient, and Africa and elsewhere.

Zionists say that only when all of the world's Jews reside in a Greater Israel will the Diaspora—the dispersion—be over.

Only then will the "wandering Jew" be returned from the "wilderness" into which he was cast. At that time, the Messiah shall come and the Jewish Utopia, global dominion by Jews, will commence.

## *Jews Living Luxuriously in Europe and America*

First, however, it is necessary for all Jews, throughout the world, to reside in Israel. The question is, since affluent and economically well-off Jews now control not only finance but also vast segments of business, education, politics and other facets of society and culture in America and Europe, what will compel the Jews living in the United States and elsewhere to resettle in Israel? Will Tom Hanks, Barbra Streisand, Larry King, Gwyneth Paltrow, Ben Bernanke, Oliver Stone, Rahm Emmanuel, Joseph Lieberman, Barbara Boxer, Ben Affleck, Barbara Walters, Tom Brokow, Bill Gates, Michael Dell, and so many other wealthy, prosperous Jews ever voluntarily leave the cushy, soft and decadent upper class lifestyles they have in the U.S.A.?

Who will force their migration to a less desirable "Israel," a nation that is first in their loyalty and in their heart, but one that also cannot provide them the fabulous advantages they possess by being the "Lords and Barons of America?" For these wealthy Jews, their "dispersion into the wilderness" of western civilization is a continuing thing of beauty and advantage. That is why there are as many Jews living in America as in Israel, even though Israel for almost seven decades has welcomed all Jews (but not Arabs or other Gentiles) with its open immigration policies.

## *World Jewry Rides the Beast*

For now, what we have is Mystery, Babylon the Great, having its feet firmly planted both in the United States and in Israel, with scattered limbs spreading into all the world. This is exactly how Bible prophecy, in *Revelation 17*, depicts the situation in

**Jews burning New Testaments and other Christian books. It has been said that burning books is a prelude to the burning of human beings.**

the last days. The Woman, the Whore of symbolic Mystery Babylon, which is World Jewry, *riding* the beast. The beast is described as "seven mountains." These are the seven continents of Earth, all the nations of this world, starting with the world's greatest superpower, the United States of America, where the majority of Jews reside.

The prophecy says that "the kings of the earth have committed fornication" with the Whore, and so they have. The Rothschilds, the Bronfmans, the Oppenheimers and all their wealthy Jewish brethren own Goldman Sachs, JP Morgan Chase, Barclays Bank, the Bank of England, Wells Fargo Bank, Morgan Stanley, HSBC Bank, and many others. The fornication of these banks through the media of money and power knows no bounds, and through their seductive power, all the world lay on their bed.

### *Affliction Number Eight: Hateful Obsession with Christianity*

The New Testament reveals that Jews are afflicted with an

overwhelming envy of Christianity and Christians and obsessed with a persistent, innate desire and urge to destroy the Christian Church and everything for which it stands.

This is understandable because it was Christ Jesus, the founder of the Christian faith, who upbraided the Pharisees—the equivalent of today's Orthodox Jews—and correctly prophesied the destruction of Jerusalem and the Jews' apostate Temple. He pointedly told the Jews, *"Therefore say I unto you, The kingdom of God shall be taken from you, and given to a nation bringing forth the fruits thereof" (Matthew 21: 43).*

The nation that replaced Israel—to whom Jesus referred—is heavenly Israel, that is, Christianity. Its citizens are born again believers in Jesus and they are called out from all ethnic groups and earthly countries to be one people, one *holy nation*. Peter spoke to Christians when he wrote:

> *"Ye also, as lively stones, are built up a spiritual house, an holy priesthood, to offer up spiritual sacrifices, acceptable to God by Jesus Christ...*
>
> *"Ye are a chosen generation, a royal priesthood, an holy nation, a peculiar people; that ye should shew forth the praises of him (Jesus) who hath called you out of darkness into his marvelous light.*
>
> *"Which in time past were not a people, but are now the people of God..."*
> —*I Peter 2:5-10*

Notice, please, that the Bible identifies Christians, not Jews and not physical Israel, as *"a chosen generation, a royal priesthood, and holy nation...the people of God."*

### The Jews' Hatred of Christianity Knows No Bounds

It is this Christian nation, this people, that the Jews are obsessed about. Judging from their own most holy book, the Talmud, their hatred for Christianity knows no bounds. In addition to the many horrendous things the Talmud says about Jesus and Mary—He is called a "sorcerer" and a "bastard," she a "whore," etc. Christians as a whole are singled out over and over with the most outrageous slanders and threats being utilized.

Among these slanders and threats:

"The pupils (students) of the recreant Jesus inherit hell." (Abot 19)

"The New Testament books of the Christians are to be burned." (Shabboth 116a)

"Whoever disobeys the rabbis deserves death and will be boiled in hot excrement in hell." (Erubin 21b)

"The worship of Jesus Christ constitutes idol worship...Idol worshippers are liable for the death penalty..." (Sanhedrin 57a; Hilchot Avodah Kachavim 9:4)

And there are more; for example, the commandment for the Jew to utter a vile curse when he passes by a Christian Church; and the duty to spit on the ground three times and grab one's crotch when passing a Christian cemetery.

### *Removing Christianity From Public View*

Their compulsive hatred for Christianity has motivated the Jewish leadership to work both clandestinely and openly to water down and diminish the Gospel message. The Jewish ADL, the ACLU, the American Jewish Congress, and many other local, national, and international groups labor incessantly to remove all vestiges of Christianity from public view and practice. The attacks include demands to eliminate prayer in schools and athletic events; the removal of Christmas displays and attempts to substitute pagan or secular symbols—bunnies and eggs and no passion plays at Easter; Santa Claus, Christmas trees, tinsel and other non-sectarian decorations for Christmas with all evidence of Jesus' birth removed.

Many public schools, thanks to Jewish lobbying and threat of lawsuits, are prohibited from even mentioning the name of Christian holidays. Quotes by America's founding fathers of praise for or belief in Christ and the Bible have been removed from school textbooks. The list of anti-Christian activities goes on and on. In every case, we find that Jews are behind these persistent attacks on the Christian faith.

In contrast, more and more public displays of the Menorah and other Jewish religious symbols are going up. The Jews—a tiny minority, some two percent of our population—demand and get equal time and space for Hanukkah, Yom Kippur, and other Jewish holy days. A gigantic Jewish Menorah is erected now once each year on the White House lawn, and inside, the First family celebrates with the Jews by observing a Sedar dinner.

Proclamations by the President honoring Christian holidays or laws are frowned upon and severely restricted by Jewish leaders, but our Congress and President George H. W. Bush signed a proclamation for the nation to observe *"Education Day U.S.A.,"* to honor the hateful, bigoted teachings of the insane "rebby" of the fanatical Lubavitcher Talmudic sect, the late Rabbi Schneerson. Amazingly, the proclamation praised the Talmud's Noahide Laws, which demand that Gentiles prove themselves "righteous" by obeying seven universal laws. One of these laws is a prohibition against idolatry. In the Talmud, as we have seen, the worship of Jesus Christ constitutes idolatry and the penalty for idol worship is death by beheading.

In passing legislation enabling the Talmud's Noahide Laws to be praised and honored as worthy and commendable, our Congress and President were, in effect, recommending that every Christian in the United States be arrested, confined, and executed by guillotine or by some other beheading method!

## *Affliction Number Nine: Pollute Christian Church From Within*

Its obsessive hatred for Christianity leads the Jews not only to attack its outward manifestation and limit public knowledge of its merits, but also to infiltrate the Church from within, thereby diminishing its effectiveness and, if possible, eventually destroying the Church altogether.

In this regard we are reminded of the Marrano Jews in Spain. When King Ferdinand and Queen Isabella in 1492 issued an edict expelling all religious Jews from the Kingdom of Spain, many Jews converted to Christianity. While they pretended to be Christians, many of these Jews continued their observance of their Talmudic Halakah (holy laws and ordinances). They also observed the Jewish high holy days and were, in truth, Christians in name only. What's more, many of the Marrano Jews, egged on in secret by rabbis, deeply resented the monarchs' expulsion order and decided to do everything in their power to destroy the Church from within. They became Sayanim, Jewish secret agents, working to pollute Christian institutions and twist Christian doctrines.

## *Jews Torturing and Executing Christians*

So successful were these infiltrators and secret agents that one of their own, the Catholic convert Tomas De Torquemada, was actually commissioned by the Pope in Rome to carry out the torture and execution of thousands of Christians accused of disloyalty to the Roman Catholic Church. Most were innocent of any actual wrongdoing, but Torquemada, historians say, prosecuted, tortured and murdered his victims with glee, inventing all sorts of new torture devices, using whips, branding irons, the rack, the Iron Maiden contraption, and so on. This was the horrific *Catholic Inquisition*, and the cruel and inhuman ghoul in charge of its chambers of horror was a Jew!

## *The Lie of Dispensationalism*

Torture and murder, however, are only mildly successful in changing mens' hearts, and the greatest success of the Jews in polluting and defeating the Christian Church lies in the Jews' poisoning and undermining the church's long-held doctrines by infusing into the Church's leadership the radical, pro-Zionist teachings of *dispensationalism*.

Dispensationalism is an unscriptural but potent doctrine which teaches the lie that the Jews, regardless of their abandonment of the Old Testament Covenant through adoption of Talmudism, and withstanding the fact that the rabbis and religious Jews reject and despise Jesus Christ and loath the Christian faith, remain eternally "God's Chosen People." Dispensationalism further instructs deceived Christians that God has made the Jews the "Apple of His eye" forever, has given them the land of "Israel" as a possession forever, and that, in the Millennium to come, the Jews will rule the entire world.

While there are some variances by its proponents, dispensational theology also generally holds that Christians are to bless Jews and modern Israel with money and political and military resources, and if they don't, God will curse them. It is also claimed by some dispensationalists —Pastor John Hagee and others—that Jews do not need to convert to Christianity to receive the Kingdom of Heaven. They can simply remain "good, faithful Jews," honoring their own religion, Judaism.

The papacy also teaches this monstrous lie, its New Catechism praising the Jews as Christians' "elder brothers" and insisting that conversion is not necessary.

## *Pastor Hagee: Jesus Is Not Messiah of the Jews*

The infamous Hagee goes so far as to preach and write that Jesus did not come as, and is not today, the "Messiah of Israel." As radical and as unorthodox as these claims of Hagee are, because the teachings of the Judaizers have been so successful over the last century, Hagee and his clones have developed a sizeable following. Hagee's pro-Zionist organization, Christians and Jews United for Israel, has a membership of over a thousand pastors and its meetings and rallies draw over 10,000 participants. This even though the name of Jesus is not uttered so that the Jews might not be offended.

Dispensational theology posits the preposterous and absurd—not to mention unholy and unbiblical—view that Christians are not God's holy nation (but see *I Peter 2:9*), are not God's Chosen People (but, again, see *I Peter 2:9* and *Galatians 3:26-29*), and are not Abraham's spiritual seed (but, see *Galatians 3:29*).

### *Dispensationalists Seek to Nullify and Defeat Christ*

Dispensationalists seek to *undo* what Christ did in prophesying (*Matthew 23*) a curse that the House of Israel would be "left desolate" until His return in glory. Instead, they support the immediate *rebuilding* of the Temple in Jerusalem, whereas Jesus had prophesied it was to be destroyed, every stone being thrown down. In sum, those who subscribe to dispensationalism are working to *nullify and defeat* Christ's wishes! They are in rebellion to God's Word; yet these millions of deceived psuedo-Christians consider themselves to be pious and holy as "lovers" of Israel.

Unpatriotic to God and country, they put the earthly nation of Israel on a pedestal. Many American dispensationalists even boast that if America and Israel were ever to clash militarily, they would choose to defend Israel and make war on America!

Dispensationalists vainly attempt to "bless national, physical Israel," imagining that in so doing, a pleased God will reward and bless them. The dispensationalists favor billions of foreign aid money be given by Washington, D.C. to support Israel. Many literally hate the Palestinians, whom they perceive to be a threat to "Holy Israel." There is no Christian sympathy in their hearts for the suffering and misery endured by the displaced Palestinian people. One well-known Baptist evangelist has even written that he would be delighted if Palestinian youth were to just lay down on the sidewalk or street and have a bullet shot into their heads by Israeli soldiers.

Obviously, this type of sentiment indicates an unacceptable satanic attitude toward humanity itself, but this comment by an evangelist whose views are no doubt shared by many other dispensationalists illustrates the hellish depths of this sinister doctrine.

## *The Follies of Cyrus Scofield*

The lie of dispensationalism first took root in Scotland in the nineteenth century but took full flight in the United States and then the rest of the Christian world in the twentieth century. It's growth accelerated after a corrupt lawyer, Cyrus Scofield, abandoning his wife and children in the midwest and fleeing charges of criminal activity, settled in New York City.

There, he somehow became acquainted with wealthy Zionist Jews, Samuel Untermyer being one of them. These Zionist activists took Scofield into their clique. He was invited and became a member of their exclusive men's fraternity, the Lotus Club, and they arranged for him to publish the Scofield Bible. This Bible edition included within its pages Scofield's commentaries on Israel and its prophetic destiny. Naturally, the commentaries of Scofield endorsed the heretical dispensationalist viewpoints and so his Zionist handlers were very pleased.

Published by Oxford, a prestigious academic publisher in Great Britain, and released with tremendous, funded publicity and fanfare, the Scofield Bible quickly became a favorite in Baptist, and later in Pentecostal, circles.

Scofield, masquerading as a born again Christian, persuaded many well-known conservative Christian pastors of his "authentic" rebirth and of his biblical sincerity. While he had no

**An anti-Germany rally in 1933 by Samuel Untermyer and Jews. The Jews in Europe and the U.S. declared war against Hitler in 1932, as soon as he was elected to office. They also worked behind the scenes to get America into the war. Untermeyer and his cronies, along with con-man "Bible" teacher Cyrus Scofield, were members of the exclusive and wealthy Lotus Club in New York City.**

theological training, Scofield's law background and the fact that the prestigious Oxford University Press had its imprimatur stamp of approval on his Scofield Bible greatly impressed the conservative Christian pastors and teachers, most of whom personally had little formal education.

Of course, these men knew nothing of Scofield's tarnished personal history and background. They did not know of his abandoning his family, of his alleged criminality and so forth. Nor were they aware of the rich Zionists, backers of Cyrus Scofield and his bible, lurking in the background.

Scofieldism swept the evangelical churches and today dispensationalism is prevalent in America's largest denominations, the Southern Baptist Convention, the Assemblies of God, the Church of God, and the United Pentecostal Church. It is also embraced by many hundreds of independent pastors, churches, and ministries.

## *Dispensationalism A Boon For Talmudic Rabbis*

Dispensationalism has proven a marvelous boon for the rabbis and their vicious Talmudic religion. With this pernicious doctrine such concepts as Jewish triumphalism and Jewish racial and spiritual superiority have become accepted doctrines of tens of millions of gullible Christians. The religion of the Jews successfully infiltrated thousands of Christian Churches and the Zionist paradigm has gained an amazingly strong foothold among the most fundamentalist and supposedly conservative of Christ groups. This has led one well-known rabbi to exclaim that, thanks to dispensationalism, "Christianity is being swallowed up by Judaism."

Dispensationalism has, sadly, today become a *cult*, a dangerous heretical cult that is antithetical to both the teachings of Jesus and the Apostles. Members of this cult studiously avoid the whole counsel of God; they omit from their reading large portions of the New Testament and purposely misinterpret many other passages of scripture.

## *Scripture Disproves Dispensationalism*

In my entire life (73 years old and counting), I have never heard one pastor preach a message using *Galatians 3:28-29* or *Revelation 2:9* and *3:9* as his proof text. These scriptures clearly disprove the lie of dispensationalism. Often, just to observe their reaction, I have presented one or all of these three fascinating and revealing passages to pastors and ministry leaders whom I count as either friends or acquaintances. Not one could explain to me the meaning of these scriptures though their meaning is self-evident! Some actually panicked and exited my presence as rapidly as they could.

For your edification, dear readers, here are the three scriptural passages that all dispensationalists studiously avoid

BLOOD COVENANT WITH DESTINY ○ 197

and which some surely wish could be stricken from the Holy Bible:

- *Galatians 3:28-29* (Christian believers in Jesus, whether Jew or Gentile are Abraham's seed and heirs to the promise):

    *"There is neither Jew nor Greek, there is neither bond nor free, there is neither male nor female: for ye are all one in Christ Jesus. And if ye be Christ's, then are ye Abraham's seed, and heirs according to the promise."*

- *Revelation 2:9* (Jesus identifies those of the Synagogue of Satan who claim to be "Jews" to be blasphemers):

    *"I know thy works, and tribulation, and poverty, (but thou art rich) and I know the blasphemy of them which say they are Jews, and are not, but are the synagogue of Satan."*

- *Revelation 3:9* (Jesus identifies those of the Synagogue of Satan who claim to be "Jews" to be purveyors of a lie):

    *"Behold, I will make them of the synagogue of Satan, which say they are Jews, and are not, but do lie; behold, I will make them to come and worship before thy feet, and to know that I have loved thee."*

True Christians will especially love the poignant and heart-stirring verses in *Revelation 2:9* and *3:9* in which Jesus our Lord and Saviour, spoke to his Apostle, John, in exile on the Island of Patmos. The book of *Revelation* is dated 95 AD, a quarter of a century after the destruction of Jerusalem and Israel by Roman General Titus in 70 AD. The prophecy speaks of the *Synagogue of Satan* and of *"them which say they are Jews, and are not, but are the synagogue of Satan."*

## False Teachers Attempt to Divert Attention

Christian Zionists and Jews despise the fact that Jesus Himself named the Synagogue of Satan as the fount of evil in the last days. Attempting to downplay these revelations, some in the Christian Church back in the 20th Century eras of Hitler and Stalin posited the theory that one or the other of these two world leaders was the Antichrist. These teachers suggested that Nazism or Communism was the last days' theology of Satan that would sweep the world, usher in the endtime plagues, and culminate in the dreadful Battle of Armegeddon. (They were, of course, unaware that the Jews had actually assisted Hitler in coming to power and that the Communist leadership in the Soviet Union was made up almost exclusively of Jews!)

## The Vatican Conquered by the Jews and Judaism

Historically, since the advent of Protestantism and Martin Luther's reformation, many Christians have insisted that the Pope was the Antichrist and his global-wide Roman Catholic Church was the Devil's endtime religious system prophesied to conquer the earth and result finally in the return of Christ.

In fact, for over a century, Rothschild, a wealthy Jew, has been the banker for the Vatican. Today, the New Catholic Catechism praises Jews as "our elder brethren in the faith." Papal encyclicals declare that Jews have their own covenant and do not need to believe in Jesus as Lord. The Pope has apologized to the Jews. In sum, the Jews have conquered the Vatican.

## Islam Falsely Accused

Now, following the 9/11 World Trade Center disaster and the ongoing military conflicts between United States forces and Moslems in Iraq, Afghanistan, Pakistan, and elsewhere in the Middle East, we find a flood of books in bookstores and teachings in Christian churches contending that Islam is the prophesied last days enemy of Christ and His church. Authors of these books, several of which have become brisk bestsellers, theorize that a cruel and satanic Moslem leader will soon rise up in the Middle East and lead all Moslems in a final *Jihad* against modern civilization and against the Christian faith.

Whereas we can surely fault Islam in many of its teachings, and Christians are called to stand against it, there is not one shred of evidence in the Word of God that Islam is to play a large prophetic role. Exactly the opposite. But this fact does not stop the opponents of Islam from capitalizing on the gullibility and fear of a huge segment of today's Christendom. Indeed giant profits are being made on the fear posed by the Islam threat.

How could all these sincere men, no doubt many of whom were and are good Christians, have overlooked the vital scriptures of prophecy which God over 1900 years ago planted directly in the body of the greatest prophetic book of all—the *Book of Revelation*? The fact that so many have neglected these prophetic passages confirms Jesus' cautionary warning that, in the last days, *"If it were possible, even the very elect would be deceived" (Matthew 24:24).*

The reality is that the vast majority of men and women who profess to be Christians regrettably have either neglected these passages, purposely discarded them, or wrongly adjudged them to be unimportant and inconsequential. What a tragic and dangerous situation!

Imagine: Jesus Christ actually identified the exact evil religious system, the Synagogue of Satan, and the Devil's human legion, *"them which say they are Jews and are not but do lie,"* as the endtime force that will in the last days confront and make war on Christians and the Christian Church. It is both distressing and remarkable that only a tiny number of Christians living today are knowledgeable or even remotely aware of these incredible prophecies of Jesus.

## Masters of Misdirection

Obviously, the Jews are masters of misdirection. Their propagandists have been successful in getting Christians to prophetically look everywhere but in the direction of the Jews and the bogus state of Israel. However, I am thrilled to report that increasingly, Christians are discovering the Truth. More and more are reading and studying the whole Word of God, including these highly descriptive passages in *Revelation*. They are waking up to the real and present danger that today confronts America and the world.

When I quote to evangelical Christian groups these passages of scripture which identify satanic Jews as the principal last days enemy of God, I almost always encounter hostility and anger. Many are incensed not only at me, but at the scriptures as well. They actually prefer to believe in the lie.

A few have come up to me after meetings and angrily insisted that I must have found these passages in the older King James Version. I respond by kindly referring the doubters to their own version, the more recently introduced versions—the NASV, RSV, etc. When they look in those versions, of course, they discover the same teachings, even if worded slightly different. They usually leave confused and bewildered, refusing to accept the very Word of God.

## Affliction Number Ten: Final Judgment of the Rebellious and Apostate Jews

We have seen so far nine afflictions that have been laid on Jews and earthly Israel due to the Jews' apostasy and rebellion. Among the afflictions is Jesus' curse that the unrepentant Jews are charged with the crime of the murder of all the righteous blood ever shed on the face of planet earth. We have seen that because of their murders and because of the unparalleled deviltry of their man-made and satanically crafted religion, Judaism, the House of Israel is "left desolate" until Jesus once again returns. We have also discovered that the Jews have been possessed by demons and turned over to Satan for destruction. Because of their extreme and insane hated of Jesus and Christians and obsession with their unattainable goal of smashing Christianity, the Jews have already been judged and their *punishment determined.*

We discover, in considering Christ's Parable of the Tares, that, in contrast to God's servants, born again Christians who have sown the good seed which is Christ, the Devil, through the ages, has sown tares, or weeds, on earth. The tares, Christ said, "are the children of the wicked one."

The enemy that sowed the tares, said Jesus, "is the devil, and the harvest is the end of the world, and the reapers of the harvest are the angels."

### Jews to Be Recompensed for Their Hatred and Wickedness

You will recall that in *Matthew 23*, Jesus forthrightly told the Jews, *"Ye are of your father the devil, and his works ye will do."* So yes, the Jews are the children of the wicked one. And upon His return, these enemies of Christ Jesus shall be recompensed for their hatred and for their wickedness.

> *"The Son of man* (Jesus) *shall send forth his angels, and they shall gather out of his kingdom all things that offend, and them which do iniquity; And shall cast them into a furnace of fire: there shall be wailing and gnashing of teeth. Then shall the righteous shine forth as the sun in the kingdom of their Father. Who hath ears to hear, let him hear."*
> —*Matthew 13:41-43*

The fate of the Jews, being prescribed in advance, is also revealed in other parables of Jesus. (Note: I include in the category of "Jews" all who, saying they are Jews, reject Jesus Christ the Messiah and stoutly hold to the Jewish quest for global supremacy.)

### *Parable of the Hateful Citizen*

Let us now examine the more pungent of these revelatory parables, considering first the Parable of the Hateful Citizens *(Luke 19:11-27)*. This parable concerns the Kingdom of Heaven and explains the fate of both the servants of God (Christians) and those who stubbornly refuse to serve the Lord Jesus Christ. Jesus teaches as follows:

> *"A certain nobleman* (Jesus) *went into a far country to receive for himself a kingdom, and to return...*
>
> *"But his citizens* (the House of Israel, the Jews) *hated him, and sent a message to him, saying, we will not have this man to rule over us...*
>
> *"And it came to pass, that when he was returned, having received the kingdom, then he commanded his servants to be called unto him..."*

At this point in the parable, Jesus rewards his faithful servants, each receiving their just due for services rendered to the nobleman and king in his absence. What, though, of those who had refused to be his servants, who pompously and callously had sent him a message, saying, "We will not have this man (Jesus) to reign over us?" Of these the nobleman, who, of truth is none other than Jesus Christ, King of Israel, commands:

> *"But those mine enemies, which would not that I should reign over them, bring hither, and slay before me."*
>
> —*Revelation 19:27*

Let no man vainly attempt to misinterpret the words of Jesus in this powerful parable. Clearly, we see that the "citizens" of this country (Israel) *hate* the nobleman. So much so that in his absence, they send a message, declaring, "We will not have this man (Jesus) reign over us."

But their unwarranted rebellion in due time brings terrible retribution to the hateful citizens in the form of a just punishment. Upon his return, the nobleman, now being made King, instructs his servants: "But these mine enemies, which would not that I reign over them, bring hither, and slay before me."

### *The Jews Have Sent Jesus A Message*

The wicked and reprobate House of Israel rejected Jesus the Messiah and after his earthly death and resurrection, they have indeed, "sent him a message." For over 1900 years they have repeated this message, in their Talmud, in their synagogues, and openly to the whole world: "We will not have this man, Jesus, reign over us." The rabbis, whether figuratively or literally, today continue to shake their fists at heaven and reject their rightful Messiah and King, Jesus. When Christ, therefore returns, He will do exactly as this Parable warns.

### *Parable of the Householder and the Vineyard*

Likewise, in the Parable of the Householder and the Vineyard, Christ remarkably delivered a similar prophetic warning:

> *"Hear another parable: There was a certain householder, which planted a vineyard, and hedged it round about, and digged a winepress in it, and built a tower, and let it out to husbandmen, and went into a far country:*
>
> *"And when the time of the fruit drew near, he sent his servants to the husbandmen, that they might receive the fruits of it.*
>
> *"And the husbandmen took his servants, and beat one, and killed another, and stoned another.*

*"Again, he sent other servants more than the first: and they did unto them likewise.*

*"But last of all he sent unto them his son, saying, They will reverence my son.*

*"But when the husbandmen saw the son, they said among themselves, This is the heir; come, let us kill him, and let us seize on his inheritance.*

*"And they caught him, and cast him out of the vineyard, and slew him.*

*"When the lord therefore of the vineyard cometh, what will he do unto those husbandmen?*

*"They say unto him, He will miserably destroy those wicked men, and will let out his vineyard unto other husbandmen, which shall render him the fruits in their seasons.*

*"Jesus saith unto them, Did ye never read in the scriptures, The stone which the builders rejected, the same is become the head of the corner: this is the Lord's doing, and it is marvellous in our eyes?*

*"Therefore I say unto you, The kingdom of God shall be taken from you, and given to a nation bringing forth the fruits thereof.*

*"And whosoever shall fall on this stone shall be broken: but on whomsoever it shall fall, it will grind him to powder.*

*"And when the chief priests and Pharisees had heard his parables, they perceived that he spake of them."*
*— Matthew 21: 33-45*

Here again is a scene depicting the Jews of the House of Israel, favored by a householder (God), being leased a valuable property on behalf of its owner and householder. That property had on its premises a vineyard. The lessors, called the "husbandmen" (the Jews), rebelliously refused to render unto the absentee householder the fruits of the vineyard which rightfully belonged to him. They even took his servants (Christians), beat one, stoned another, and killed yet another.

The householder sent more servants, but the selfish and cruel lessors (the Jews) did the same terrible things to them. Lastly, the householder (God) sent unto them his own son, reasoning, "Surely, they will reverence my son."

But the greedy, evil husbandmen saw the son and conspired against him, saying, "Come, let us kill him and seize on his inheritance."

"And they caught him, and cast him out of the vineyard, and slew him."

Is this not exactly a mirror image of what the Jews did to

"But last of all he sent unto them his son, saying, They will reverence my son. But when the husbandmen saw the son, they said among themselves. This is the heir; come, let us kill him, and let us seize on his inheritance. And they caught him, and cast him out of the vineyard, and slew him." *(Matthew 21:33-45)*

Jesus the Son of God? Rabbinical leaders in Jerusalem conspired. They knew that Jesus was the rightful heir to the Kingdom. They said, "Come, let us kill him, and let us seize on his inheritance."

Bribing Judas to betray Jesus, they indeed "caught him," cast him out of the vineyard, had the Roman soldiers take him to a hill named Golgotha ("place of the skull") and crucified him.

The analogy is this: That the Jews are *not* the rightful heirs of the land of Israel. They are not heirs to the kingdom. They are instead *usurpers*. Yet, arrogantly, today we find World Jewry, the Jews of all the earth, claiming the ancient land of Palestine to be their *divine inheritance*! These usurpers of the Kingdom have been so audacious as to murder and imprison others (the Palestinians) whom they drove off the land. In committing these awful crimes, their accomplices, the governments of the U.S.A, Britain, France, Germany, and other nations, must also share in the judgment to come.

The evangelical Zionist Christians, including the largest non-Catholic denominations as well as the Rome-based Catholic Church and its Pontiff, are also complicit in these great crimes and are in rebellion against God, and they, too, will suffer the judgment of God.

What say the scriptures?—

*"When the Lord therefore of the vineyard cometh, what will he do unto those husbandmen? They say unto him, He will miserably destroy those wicked men..."*
　　　　　　　　　　　　　　　*—Matthew 21:41*

World Jewry, rebellious nations of the world, defiant "Christian" Judaizers: Are You Listening? Do you have ears to hear what the Spirit saith?

# INDEX

**Symbols**

666  25, 26, 27, 28, 64, 107
666 talents of gold  28, 109

**A**

Abaddon  57, 61, 66, 67
Abomination of Desolation  178
Abraham  73, 74
Abraham's seed  176, 197
ACLU (American Civil Liberties Union)  189
adepts  89
ADL (Anti-defamation De  52, 189
adultery  170
advent of Jesus  31
Affleck, Ben  186
AIPAC (American Israel Public Affairs Committee)  52
alcoholism  51
Alexander the Great  58
all seeing eye  143
Alpha and Omega  73
American Jewish Congress  189
Angel of Light  27
Antichrist  64, 103, 106, 121
Apollyon  57, 61
Apple of his eye  192
As Above, So Below  30, 55
ascendant triangle  30
Asherah poles  109
Ashkenazi  81, 162, 184
Assembly of God  154, 195
Assissi  150
Astrology  169
Attila the Hun  58, 106

**B**

Babylon  51, 84, 155, 159, 173
Babylonian Godhead  109
Babylonian numerology  25
Babylonian Talmud  50, 92, 94, 110, 124, 175
Babylon the Great  135, 172, 186
Bakst, Rabbi Joel  49, 52, 55
Baphomet  113
Battle of Armageddon  198
Bavaria  143
Begin, Menachem  154
beheaded  104
Behemoth  63
Belshazzar  110
Benjamin, Judah P.  170
Bernanke, Ben  186
bestiality  170
best of the Gentiles — kill  96
Beyond Babylon  159
Binah  30, 31
Black, Edwin  185
Black Magic  90
Blazing Star  32
Blessed Hope of Israel  162

blessing the Jews  118
blind guides  164
Bloomberg, Mayor Michael  98
Bolshevik Jews  58
Bolshevism  24
*Book of Knowledge* (book)  97
bottomless pit  60
Boxer, Barbara  186
bright and morning star  32
Brokow, Tom  186
Bronstein, Lev  147
Bush, George W.  88, 98
Bush, President George H. W.  190

**C**

Cain  171
Cardinal Augustin Bea  151
Cardinal Ratzinger  148
Catholic Church  29
Catholic Inquisition  191
*Cauldron of Abaddon* (video by Texe Marrs)  170
ceremonial magic  89
chaos magic  26
Chekhov  59
chelas  89
Chiun  51
Chokmah  30, 31
chosen generation  80, 188
Christians and Jews United for Israel  193
Christian Talmud  154
Church of God  195
Church of Satan  85, 169
Church of the Apocalypse  153
Clinton, President Bill  83, 98, 105
Code of Hell  86
*Codex Magica* (book by Texe Marrs)  83
Cohen, Moshe David Ben Schmuel

Ha  26
College of Cardinals  155
comets  29
Communism  51
Conference of the Holy See Commission for Religious Relations with Jewry  150
Constantine  139
copraphilia  170
Cornerstone Church  100
Council on Foreign Relations (CFR)  52
Covenant  74
Curse of Cain  163

**D**

Daniel  110, 125
Daniel (prophet)  167, 179
Davening  52
David, King  113
Dell, Michael  186
Delta" star  30
desolate  79, 178
Diaspora  30, 112, 185
Dispensationalism  192, 196
Dispensationalists  193
divination  169
Divine Force  31
Divine Presence  55
*DNA Science and the Jewish Bloodline* (book by Texe Marrs)  81
Dome of the Rock  121
double-headed white and black eagle  85
doubleminded  49, 50, 63

**E**

Easter  190
ecumenical movement  133

effendi 94, 96, 104
Egypt 84
Ein Sof 31, 86
Eleazar, Ben 154
Emmanuel (Jesus) 76
Emmanuel, Rahm 186
Erubin 21b 96
esoteric wisdom 54
establishment of Inner Circles 52
Eternal City 65
European-American Evangelistic Association 141
Ezekiel 110, 112

## F

Falling Away 133
Father of Lights 32
Federal Reserve System 184
fifth angel 57, 60
fifth column 144
First Cause 127
five-pointed symbol 32
Freemasonry 85
French Revolution 142
fusing with God's Presence 55
fusion 55

## G

Galilee 119
Gates, Bill 186
Gematria 109
General Titus 64, 180, 197
generative force 30
Genghis Khan 58, 106
Gibbon, Edward 182
Gingrich, Newt 83
Ginsburg, Justice Ruth Bader 124, 125
Gipp, Dr. Samuel 100

goat 113
God of Forces 32
God's Chosen People 192
golden cup 132
Golgotha 67
Gorbachev, Mikhail 105
goyim 104
Goyyah 96
Graham, Billy 155
Graham, Franklin 155
Great City 173, 174
Greater Israel Empire 24
G" symbol in Freemasonry 30
guillotine 54
*Gulag Archipelago* (book) 59
Gurion, David Ben 154

## H

Hagee, John 99, 155, 192, 193
Halakah 92, 110, 191
Hanks, Tom 186
Hanukkah 190
Hasidim 98
Hatanya 98
Hatikvah 83
Hayesod, Rabbi Moses 64
Heavenly Jerusalem 68, 71
Hebrew University 98, 125
Hegelian dialectic 88
Hendrie, Edward 135, 136
Herod, King 112
Herod's Temple 180, 184
Heydrich 185
Higger, Rabbi Michael 92, 93, 104
Hilton, Paris 83
Himmler, Heinrich 185
Hitler, Adolf 184, 185, 198
Hoffman, Michael 49, 50
holocaust 149
Holy Blessed One 128

Holy City  178
Holy Land  178
Holy One  55
Holy See  155
Holy Serpent  32, 33, 52, 53, 62, 63
Holy Serpent Kingdom  26
*Holy Serpent of the Jews* (book by Texe Marrs)  58, 61
Horus  158
householder  203, 205
House of Israel  76, 82, 155, 172, 175, 177, 193, 200
House of the Temple  114, 115
Howitt, Mary  91
husbandmen  77, 203

**I**

Ignatius Loyola  141
Illuminati  87
Imperial Rome  112
Independent Baptists  100
inferiority of the Gentiles  50
ingathering of the exiles  29
inheritance  77
Irgun  24
Isaiah (prophet)  175
Isis  158
Islam  117
Israel  57, 73
Israel of God  162
*Is the Pope Catholic?* (video by Texe Marrs)  147
Italy  150

**J**

Jackson, Michael  83, 85
Jacob  31
Jeremiah  110, 125
Jerusalem  24, 65, 67, 68, 69, 71, 79, 80, 116, 171, 174, 177, 183

*Jerusalem Post, The* (newspaper)  94
Jesuit  86
Jesuit Order  88, 142
*Jewish Encyclopedia, The* (book)  97
Jewish feasts and holy days  83
*Jewish Fundamentalism in Israel* (book)  125
*Jewish History, Jewish Religion: The Weight of Three Thousand Years* (book)  51, 121, 125, 126
Jewish Messiah  121
Jewish Mysteries  28
Jewish Supremacism  100, 154
Jewish Utopia  134
*Jewish Utopia, The* (book)  92, 93, 95
Jews do not need Jesus  135
Jihad  199
John (apostle)  197
*Judaism Discovered* (book)  49, 50
Judeo-Christianity  130

**K**

Kabbalah  27, 32, 53, 54, 58, 62, 63, 83, 84, 85, 113, 125, 154, 158, 169
Kaczorowski/Katz, Emily  146
Kapner, Nathanael  52
Katz, Emily  145
Kennedy, John F.  105
Kerry, John  88
Kether  31
Khazaria  81
Khazars  162
Kibbutz Golios  29, 30
Kiddushin 66e  96
Kingdom of Zion  95
King Ferdinand  191
King, Larry  186
King Midas  168
King of Israel  31
King Solomon  27, 28

King, Stephen  83
Kissinger, Henry  105
Kluger, Jerzy  144, 149
Knights of Kadosh  85
Kochav  32
Koestler, Arthur  81
Kol HaTor  52

**L**

Ladd, Diane  83
Laden, Osama bin  105
Lake of Fire  107
Lamb's book of life  71
Land, Richard  155
LaVey, Anton Szandor  169
Lazarus  166
Lenin, Vladimir  106, 142, 147, 155
Leviathan  32, 63, 113, 159
Lieberman, Joseph  186
London  173
Loyola, Ignatius  140, 142
Lubavitchers  98
Lucifer  27, 29, 32, 101
*Lumen 2000* (video by Texe Marrs)  147
Lustiger, Cardinal Jean  155
Luther, Martin  133, 198

**M**

Maclaine, Shirley  85
Madonna  83, 85
magic  89
Maimonidean Code  97
Maimonides, Rabbi  97, 154
male is the rising  30
mammon  166, 167
Man of Sin  121, 181
Mao  58
Margolis, Michael  26, 27, 29, 30, 32

Marrano Jews  141, 191
Marx, Karl  86, 155
Masonic Lodge  32, 52
Mausos, King  114
McCain, Senator John  99
Meah Shearim  23, 24, 25
Mecca  117
Merkaz Hárav  94
Messiah  29
Messianic (Christian) Jews  126
messianic revelation  54
Metatron  54
Mirabeau  86
Mohammed  117
Moloch  51, 158
moneychangers  112
*Morals and Dogma* (book)  85, 114, 169
Mosque of Omar  180
Mother of Harlots  131, 132, 133
Mystery Babylon  58, 76, 80
Mystery, Babylon the Great  132, 135, 186

**N**

Nazism  51
Nebuchadnezzar  110
necromancy  169
necrophilia  170
Netanyahu, Benjamin  93, 94
New Covenant  75
new King David  164
New World Order  88
Niddah  96
Nimoy, Leonard  84
Nimrod  58
Noahide Laws  54, 96, 120, 190
Nostra Aetate (papal bull)  149, 151, 152, 153, 154
Nostradamus  104

Novak, Dr. David  119
Number of the Beast  25
numerology  25, 169

## O

Obama, President  179
occult magicians  89
Ohr Somayach  25
Old Covenant  74, 150, 175, 176
Old Testament  126
Opus Dei  88
Order of Skull and Bones  87
Order of the Ages  86
Order of the Illuminati  143
oroboros  33, 62, 86
Orthodox Jews  124
Orthodox Judaism  25
Osiris  158
Osteen, Joel  155
oversoul  54
Oxford University Press  194

## P

Palestine  24, 185
Palestinians  24, 54, 99, 193
Palin, Sarah  179
Paltrow, Gwyneth  186
*Paranoia* (magazine)  83
path to initiation  32
Paul (apostle)  180
pederasty  170
pedophilia  51, 170
pentagram  32, 113
Pentecostal churches  154
perdition  132
Perez, Shimon  154
Phallic Cult  123
Pike, Albert  85, 114, 169
Pilate  77

Pinay, Maurice  144
*Plot Against the Church, The* (book)  144
Pontius Pilate  119
Pope Benedict XVI  31, 148, 151, 152, 155
Pope Francis  135, 152, 153
Pope, Mr. John  114
Pope John Paul II  29, 118, 146, 147, 148, 149, 151, 152, 153, 155
Pope Paul VI  153
Pope Benedict XVI  153
power of the Star  32
Priory of Zion  87
promised son of peace  29
*Protocols of the Learned Elders of Zion, The* (book)  92
pyramid  143

## Q

Quatrains  104
Queen Isabella  191

## R

radiant power  29
Ratzinger, Cardinal  155
Reagan, Presidents  98
rectification  54
red cross  85
redeemer initiate  32
red wristband  84
Reformation  133
Reid, Harry  83, 84
Remphan  158
righteous gentile  30, 54
Rio de Janeiro  173
*Rise and Fall of the Roman Empire* (book)  182
ritual magic  90

Ritual murder 50
Rockefeller, David 83
Roman Catholic Church 133, 135, 141, 155
Roosevelt, President Franklin D. 184
Rosen, Rabbi David 150, 151, 153
Rosicrucianism 85
Rothschild 24, 64, 198
royal priesthood 80, 188

**S**

Sanhedrin 100, 148
Sanhedrin 57a 96
Sanhedrin 81b and 82a 96
Sanhedrin 98b 95
Sanhedrin 105a 95
Santa Claus 190
Satan like lightning 27
Saturn 86
Sayanim 191
Scalia, Antonin 124
Schneerson, Rabbi Mendel M. 98, 190
Schumer, Charles 83
Schwarzenegger, Arnold 98
Scofield Bible 194
Scofield, Cyrus 194, 195
Scottish Rite Freemasonry 87, 114
Scottish Rite Lodge 85
Seal of Solomon 30
*Secret Doctrine of the Gaon of Vilna (Volume 1)* (book) 49
Serpent 62, 82
seven mountains 65, 187
Sex Gods 123
Sex magic 50
sexual coitus 30
sexual initiation 27

Sexual intercourse with children 50
Shahak, Dr. Israel 51, 98, 125, 126, 127, 130
Shanghai 173
Shas political party 93
Shekinah 31, 52, 55, 61, 127, 128
Shekinah Presence 58
Shema Yisrael 32
Shifchah 96
shin 84
six levels 55
six-pointed star 32, 51, 62, 86
Skull and Bones Society 52, 88
slashing of the throat 84
slaves for the Jews 94
Sodom and Egypt 67, 68, 137
Sodom and Gomorrah (movie) 172
sodomy 170
Solar Logos 27
Solar Root 666 26
Solomon 109, 114
*Solving the Mystery of Babylon the Great* (book) 135, 143
Solzhenitsyn 59, 60
Son of man 110
Son of Perdition 104, 106, 115, 121, 181, 182
Sorcery 169
Southern Baptist Convention 195
Southern Baptists 154
Soviet Russia 58
Spanish Inquisition 141
Spears, Britney 83
*Spider and the Fly, The* (poem) 91
Spirit of God 178
Spirit of Money 165
Spirit of Prophecy 73, 108, 174
Stalin, Josef 106, 198
Starhawk, Miriam 169
Star of David 30
star scepter 32

*Star Trek* (TV series) 84
Stephen (martyr) 51, 156
Stone, Oliver 186
St. Peter's Basilica 133
Streisand, Barbra 83, 186
Sumaria 173
Sun 27
Sun deity 29
superiority of the Jews 50
Supreme Mother 113
Supreme Mother Council 114
Synagogue of Satan 58, 81, 106, 107, 108, 134, 162, 197, 198, 199

**T**

Talmud 95, 97, 124, 163, 169, 183, 189, 203
Talmudic Judaism 95, 147
Talmudic Law 92
Talmudic traditions 164
Tammuz 111
tantric sex 55
tares 201
tarot cards 169
Tel Aviv 86
Temple Mount 116, 117
Temple of Herod 116
Ten Afflictions 163
*Thirteenth Tribe, The* (book) 81
thunderbolt 27
Tikkun 54
Tikkun Olam 26, 30, 91, 92
Titus, General 112
Torah 25
Torquemada, Tomas De 141, 142, 191
Torrell, John 141
*Tower of Infamy* (video by Texe Marrs) 147
Traditions of the Elders 164

*Transfer Agreement, The* (book) 185
Tree of Life 26, 30, 52, 53, 58, 62, 85, 176
triangle 51
Trinity Broadcasting Network 99
triple goddess 109
Trotsky, Leon 86, 142, 147
Truman, President Harry 184
Tu B'Shevat 32
two witnesses 66, 67

**U**

United Pentecostal Church 195
University of Virginia 119
Untermyer, Samuel 184, 194

**V**

Vatican 153
vav 26
Vicar of Christ 142
Vilna Gaon 25
Vulcan greeting 84

**W**

Wadowice, Poland 144
Wailing Wall 68, 117
Walters, Barbara 186
wandering Jews 30
Warren, Rick 155
Washington 114
Weishaupt, Adam 86, 141, 142, 143
whited sepulchers 164
White House 114
Wilson, President Woodrow 184
wisdom lineage 32
Wise, Rabbi Stephen 184
Wise, Yaakov 146
witch's hexagram 32

Wojtyla, Karol  144, 145, 146
World Jewry  82, 162, 163

## Y

Yale University  87
Yeshivas  124
Yom Kippur  190
Yosef, Rabbi Ovadia  93, 94

## Z

Zionism  51
Zohar  29, 30, 84
Zonah  96

# ABOUT THE AUTHOR

Well-known author of the #1 national bestseller, *Dark Secrets of The New Age*, Texe Marrs has written books for such major publishers as Simon & Schuster, John Wiley, Prentice Hall/Arco, McGraw-Hill, and Dow Jones-Irwin. His books have sold millions of copies. He is one of the world's foremost symbologists and is a first-rate scholar of ancient history and Mystery religions.

Texe Marrs was assistant professor of aerospace studies, teaching American defense policy, strategic weapons systems, and related subjects at the University of Texas at Austin for five years. He has also taught international affairs, political science, and psychology for two other universities. A graduate *summa cum laude* from Park College, Kansas City, Missouri, he earned his Master's degree at North Carolina State University.

As a career USAF officer (now retired), he commanded communications-electronics and engineering units. He holds a number of military decorations including the Vietnam Service Medal and Presidential Unit Citation, and has served in Germany, Italy, and throughout Asia.

President of RiverCrest Publishing in Austin, Texas, Texe Marrs is a frequent guest on radio and TV talk shows throughout the U.S.A. and Canada. His monthly newsletter, *Power of Prophecy*, is distributed around the world, and he is heard globally on his popular, international shortwave and internet radio program, *Power of Prophecy*. His articles and research are published regularly on his exclusive websites: *powerofprophecy.com* and *conspiracyworld.com*.

Texe Marrs is also pastor and host of *Bible Home Church*. You may listen to Bible Home Church 24/7 on website *www.biblehomechurch.org*.

## FOR OUR NEWSLETTER

*Power of Prophecy* offers a free sample copy of our newsletter focusing on world events, false religion, and secret societies, cults, and the occult challenge to Christianity. If you would like to receive this newsletter, please write to:

Power of Prophecy<br>
1708 Patterson Road<br>
Austin, Texas 78733

You may also e-mail your request to:<br>
customerservice1@powerofprophecy.com

## FOR OUR WEBSITE

*Power of Prophecy's* newsletter is published free monthly on our website. This website has descriptions of all Texe Marrs' books, and are packed with interesting, insight-filled articles, videos, breaking news, and other information. You also have the opportunity to order an exciting array of books, tapes, and videos through our online Catalog and Sales Stores. Visit our website at:

www.powerofprophecy.com<br>
www.conspiracyworld.com

## OUR RADIO PROGRAM

*Power of Prophecy's* international radio program, *Power of Prophecy*, is broadcast weekly on shortwave radio throughout the United States and the world. *Power of Prophecy* can be heard on WWCR at 4.840 Sunday nights at 9:00 p.m. Central Time. You may also listen to *Power of Prophecy* 24/7 on website *www.powerofprophecy.com*.

## MORE RESOURCES FOR YOU

**Books:**

**(For all orders, please include shipping and handling charge)**

**Bloody Zion—Refuting the Jewish Fables That Sustain Israel's War Against God and Man**, by Edward Hendrie (544 pages) $28.00

**Conspiracy of the Six-Pointed Star—Eye Opening Revelations and Forbidden Knowledge About Israel, the Jews, Zionism, and the Rothschilds**, by Texe Marrs (432 pages) $25.00

**Codex Magica—Secret Signs, Mysterious Symbols, and Hidden Codes of the Illuminati**, by Texe Marrs (624 pages) $35.00

**Conspiracy World—A Truthteller's Compendium of Eye-Opening Revelations and Forbidden Knowledge**, by Texe Marrs (432 pages) $25.00

**The Destroyer—The Antichrist Is At Hand**, by Texe Marrs (96 pages) $20.00

**DNA Science and the Jewish Bloodline**, by Texe Marrs (256 pages) $20.00

**Feast of the Beast**, by Texe Marrs (96 pages) $15.00

**Gods of the Lodge**, by Reginald Haupt (195 pages) $15.00

**Hell's Mirror—Global Empire of the Illuminati Builders**, by Texe Marrs (224 pages) $25.00

**Judaism's Strange Gods**, by Michael Hoffman (381 pages) $22.00

**Matrix of Gog—From the Land of Magog Came the Khazars to Destroy and Plunder**, by Daniel Patrick (160 pages) $18.00

**Mysterious Monuments—Encyclopedia of Secret Illuminati Designs, Masonic Architecture, and Occult Places**, by Texe Marrs (624 pages) $35.00

**On the Jews and Their Lies,** by Martin Luther (240 pages) $20.00

**Protocols of the Learned Elders of Zion** (320 Pages) $20.00

Videos:

**Cauldron of Abaddon**—"From Jerusalem and Israel Flow a Torrent of Satanic Evil and Mischief Endangering the Whole World" (DVD) $25.00

**Illuminati Mystery Babylon**—The Hidden Elite of Israel, America, and Russia, and Their Quest for Global Dominion (DVD) $25.00

**Invasion of Israel: The Matrix of Gog,** by Daniel Patrick (DVD) $25.00

**Masonic Lodge Over Jerusalem** —The Hidden Rulers of Israel, the Coming World War in the Middle East, and the Rebuilding of the Temple (DVD) $25.00

**Thunder Over Zion**—Illuminati Bloodlines and the Secret Plan for A Jewish Utopia and a New World Messiah (DVD) $25.00

---

Shipping in the USA: Orders up to $50, please add $5 shipping.
Orders over $50, please add 10% for shipping.
Canadian Orders: 50% shipping, $17 minimum.
All Other Foreign Orders: 70% shipping, $25 minimum.

Visa/Mastercard/Discover/American Express Accepted

To order, www.powerofprophecy.com, or
Phone 1-800-234-9673 or 1-512-263-9780,
or send check or money order to: Power of Prophecy
1708 Patterson Road, Austin, Texas 78733

Check Out This Web Site for more invaluable
books, videos, audiotapes, and for breaking news and informative
articles: www.powerofprophecy.com

# The Truth About Israel, the Jews, and Zionism

**432 Power-packed pages by Texe Marrs**

$25 Plus S&H

In *Conspiracy of the Six-Pointed Star* discover eye-opening revelations and forbidden knowledge about Rothschild, Israel, the Jews, and Zionism, and the hidden agenda that propels these evil forces. Greed, money, murder, and blood—these are the inflammable factors that motivate the elite, and you'll find out just how horribly dark-hearted these Luciferian conspirators are. Unbelievable? Well, you won't think so after you have read the astonishing, documented facts revealed in this riveting, groundbreaking book.

**Order Now! Phone toll free 1-800-234-9673**
Or send your check or money order to
RiverCrest Publishing ~ 1708 Patterson Rd, Austin, TX 78733

# DNA Science Has Unraveled the Jewish Bloodline

*A groundbreaking tour de force!*
*By Texe Marrs ~ 256 pages*

DNA science joins recent discoveries in history and archaeology to present the world with a correct and remarkable picture of the Jewish people. DNA confirms that today's "Jews" are not descendants of Abraham but are, in fact, of Turkic bloodline. *Now, everything changes!*

**Order Now! Phone toll free 1-800-234-9673**
Or send your check or money order to
RiverCrest Publishing ~ 1708 Patterson Rd, Austin, TX 78733

# Unmasking the Most Colossal Devil Religion Ever

**The Rabbis' Secret Plan for Satan to Crush Their Enemies and Vault the Jews to Global Dominion**

## Holy Serpent of the Jews

### TEXE MARRS

*$20 Plus S&H*

*"Discover the Rabbis' Secret Plan for Satan to Crush Their Enemies and Vault the Jews to Global Dominion"* —Texe Marrs

On the surface, the Jews appear to be pious, humanitarian, charitable, and good. The very picture of saintly human beings, they are said to be exalted and true, God's Chosen.

But appearances are deceiving. The evil spirits of those who once worshipped Moloch, who fashioned a golden calf in the desert, and who tortured and tormented Jesus Christ are back, and the whole world is in jeopardy. Making its way on stage is the most colossal devil religion ever. The People of the Serpent have awakened Abaddon and the Beast is rising.

**Order Now! Phone toll free 1-800-234-9673**
Or send your check or money order to
RiverCrest Publishing ~ 1708 Patterson Rd, Austin, TX 78733

# Texe Marrs' Newest Exposés

*"Who is a liar but he that denieth that Jesus is the Christ? He is antichrist, that denieth the Father and the Son."*
—I John 2:22

For over 2,000 years our forefathers whispered in awed tones that he was coming. Now, the Destroyer is at hand. He will declare himself God and above every other god. He will make war on the Saints. He will begin by rising from the pit of hell in that Great City, Jerusalem, known spiritually as Sodom and Egypt. In the hebrew tongue, his name is *Abaddon* ("The Destroyer) and in the Greek, *Apollyon*. Christians will simply know him as *Antichrist*. He must move fast for his time is short. Soon, he knows, he, the Destroyer, will in his turn be *destroyed*.

**192 Page Book by Texe Marrs**
**$20 (plus $5 s&h)**

---

This is the first book written for both Gentiles and Jews which fully explains the doctrines of kabbalistic Judaism pertaining to the events of the Last Days. Kabbalistic Judaism teaches that when the Messiah of the Jews comes, the Jews will universally celebrate the Feast of the Beast. This will be a time of great joy as their Messiah promotes the Jews to godhood. The Earth and its riches shall be the sole heritage of the divine Jewish race. And exactly who is this Messiah who will promote the Jews to godhood and elevate them to global power while smiting the Gentiles? The Jewish Kabbalah tells us his name. You will be both shocked and dismayed to discover his identity.

**96 Page Book by Texe Marrs**
**$15 (plus $5 s&h)**

## Order Now! Phone toll free 1-800-234-9673
Or send your check or money order to

# Global Empire of the Illuminati Builders

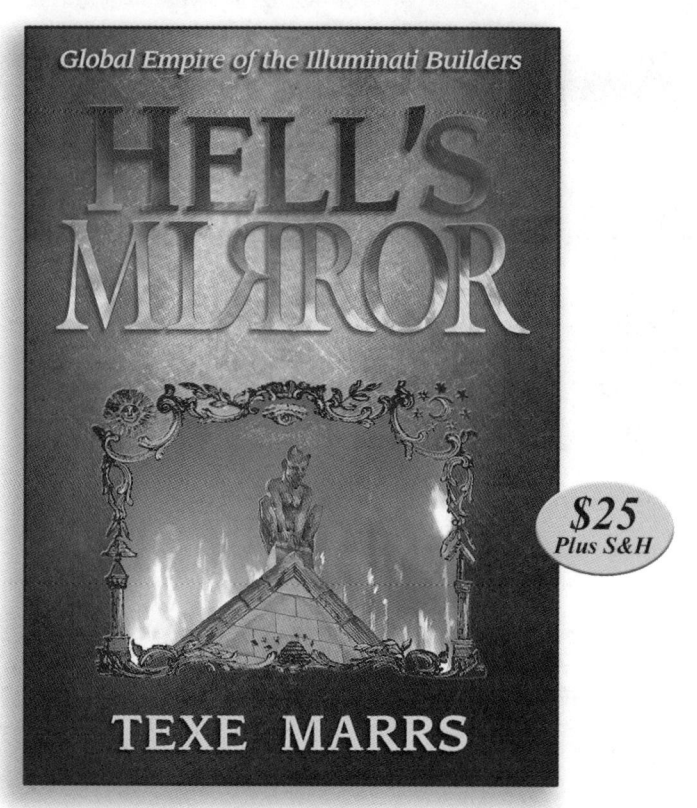

**$25 Plus S&H**

## Exposes the Double-Minded Illuminists!
### By Texe Marrs ~ Large Format ~ 256 pages

Who are the Illuminati Builders? Why do they seek and plan a Global Empire? Why do they hate and despise America and Christianity? What is the philosophy of the Illuminati? What is their New Reality? How do they keenly employ a serpentine vision of doublemindedness? How do they use the "seething energies of Lucifer?" Do they possess a "Holy Madness?" Do they worship the Great Serpent? What of their Ancient Lost Religion and their fascination with death? Will they succeed in their unholy quest and thus fulfill Prophecy?

### Order Now! Phone toll free 1-800-234-9673
Or send your check or money order to
RiverCrest Publishing ~ 1708 Patterson Rd, Austin, TX 78733